The AI-Driven Leader

The AI-Driven Leader

Harnessing AI to Make Faster, Smarter Decisions

Geoff Woods

JOHN MURRAY BUSINESS

Published in the US by Authors Equity in 2026
Previously published in 2024 by AI Thought Leadership™

First published in Great Britain by John Murray Business in 2026
An imprint of John Murray Publishing Group

1

The acknowledgments constitute an extension of this copyright page.

A CIP catalogue record for this title is available from the British Library

Hardback ISBN 9781399843461
Trade Paperback ISBN 9781399843478
ebook ISBN 9781399843485

Printed and bound in Great Britain by Clays Ltd, Elcograf S.p.A.

John Murray Publishing Group policy is to use papers that are natural, renewable and recyclable products and made from wood grown in sustainable forests. The logging and manufacturing processes are expected to conform to the environmental regulations of the country of origin.

John Murray Publishing Group
Carmelite House
50 Victoria Embankment
London EC4Y 0DZ

www.johnmurraybusiness.com

John Murray Publishing Group, part of Hodder & Stoughton Limited
An Hachette UK company

The authorised representative in the EEA is Hachette Ireland, 8 Castlecourt Centre, Dublin 15, D15 XTP3, Ireland (email: info@hbgi.ie)

To my incredible wife, Amy, and our amazing children, Daphne, Dean, and Aspen. Your support and belief in me have made all the difference. This book is for you.

Table of Contents

PART 3
BUILD AN AI-DRIVEN ORGANIZATION

Part One

Redefine Your Leadership in the AI Era

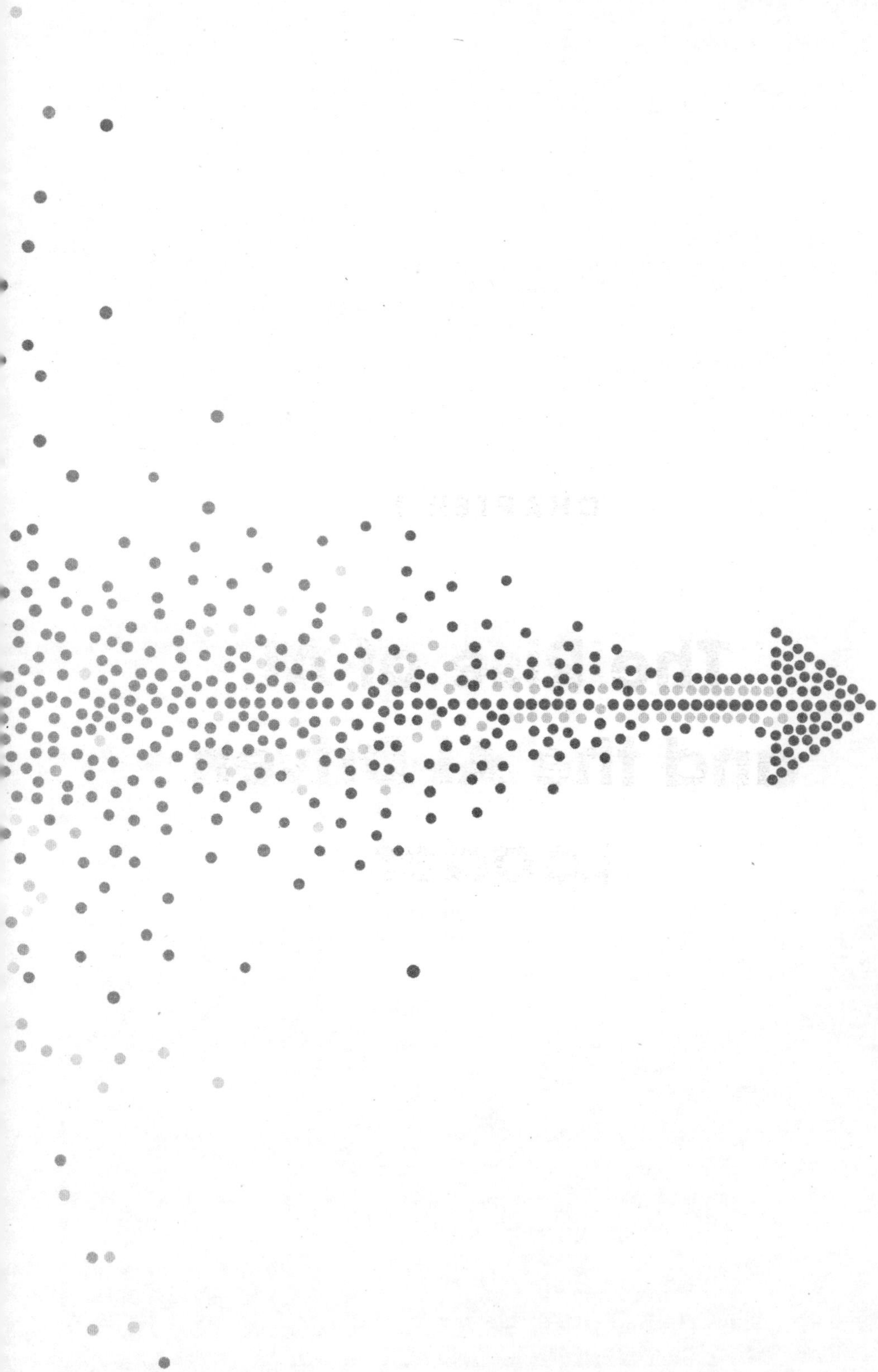

CHAPTER 1

The Rise of AI and the AI-Driven Leader

"We're going bankrupt, and there's nothing I can do to stop it."

The businessman across from me looked exhausted. He wore a crisp collared shirt and sat with a stiff posture, but his face gave him away. He was worried. *Really* worried.

It was mid-2024, and I was speaking at a YPO (Young Presidents' Organization) forum in Austin, Texas. Eight business leaders were gathered around a table, eager to learn how AI could help their companies.

I sat down and asked them a question: "What are the biggest problems you're facing in your business right now that, if we could solve them, would unlock a completely new level of growth for you?"

The question was strategic. I don't care about AI; I care about helping people build better businesses and better lives. I wanted them to focus on what truly mattered.

The man exhaled sharply and looked at me. "I've got one for you. I run a manufacturing company. I leased all the capital equipment from another company in Japan, but things have shifted in the market. Now, the debt is killing us. If we don't get the debt restructured, we'll go bankrupt."

In my mind, I thought, *Is this a 20% problem? If we solve it, could it drive 80% of the results?* The answer was a resounding yes.

I looked at him and asked, "What have you tried so far?"

He sighed. "Everything."

He then listed off five specific strategies he had attempted. Then he looked at me and said, "None of this has worked because this is a public company in Japan. It's gone all the way to the board, and they are refusing to restructure the debt because they think they will lose face in Japanese society."

He took a deep breath, and said, "I have no next steps. We're probably going out of business." Then he paused and asked *"Can AI help me?"*

This was the right question.

So many of us go through life facing problems and asking, *How can I do this?* without realizing that we have a new thought partner at our fingertips. This partner can expand what's possible for all of us. All we have to do is ask, *How can AI help me do this?*

I opened up ChatGPT and wrote a very strategic prompt using my favorite framework: Context, Role, Interview, Task. Here was the exact prompt:

> CONTEXT: I'm the CEO of a manufacturing company. I leased all this capital equipment from a company in Japan. Things have shifted in the market. The debt is now killing us. We're going to go bankrupt if it doesn't get restructured. I feel like we've tried everything.

Then I listed the five strategies he had outlined.

> None of it has worked because this is a public company in Japan. It's gone all the way to the board, and they are refusing to restructure the debt because they think they'll lose face in Japanese society. I have no next steps, and we're probably going out of business.
>
> YOUR ROLE: Act as an investment banker with deep expertise in restructuring debt.
>
> INTERVIEW ME: Ask me one question at a time, up to three questions, to gain deeper context so that you can accomplish the task.
>
> TASK: Generate five non-obvious strategies I could deploy to get the board to restructure the debt.

Instead of asking AI a question and getting an average answer, we turned the tables—AI began to interview us. It started with a very pointed question:

> "Do you have relationships with any other influential executives in Japan that the board would respect?"

I looked at the CEO, and he was shocked.

"Wow," he said. "I would have never asked that question. What a great question." Then he turned to me with a smile and said, "I actually do!"

In that moment, I realized—he didn't have centuries of Japanese cultural context in his head. But AI did. And that's why it asked the question he never would have thought to.

Then it asked two more surgical questions just like that and came back with five non-obvious strategies.

The first was called "The Saving Face Consortium."

It said:

> "You have enough relationships with the right people in Japan. Approach them to acquire the debt, give them really favorable terms. Your debt will get restructured, and your board will save face."

I looked at him, and his whole body language shifted.

He was on the verge of tears. He looked at the people in his forum and, very vulnerably, said, "I haven't slept in 90 days. I have literally been making peace with the fact that we are going out of business. And in less than 10 minutes," he pointed to the screen, "I've got hope."

We kept in touch over the next few months. I'll never forget the day he sent me this message:

"The ball is moving, and I actually think this is going to get done."

The difference between growing your business or going out of

business lies in your ability to think strategically. The question is, how do you make faster, smarter decisions?

That's what this book will answer.

Why Brilliant Leaders Still Fail at Strategic Thinking

Every leader understands the importance of strategic thinking. That's not an exaggeration. A survey of 10,000 senior leaders by the Management Research Group and published in the *Harvard Business Review* found that **97% believed strategic thinking was the number-one most important leadership behavior for their organization's future success.**

What Is Strategic Thinking?

> The process of defining your strategy, then aligning your actions to achieve your most ambitious goals. This critical skill is the backbone of effective leadership, and the difference between you becoming a visionary leader, or a mere manager.

The problem? Leaders don't have enough time to do it. I'm guessing that's probably your situation as well. Does this sound familiar?

- Your calendar looks like a chaotic game of Tetris, with barely a moment to breathe.
- You're often stuck in operational tasks, overwhelmed by never-ending to-do lists.
- Endless distractions, like phone notifications and countless emails, fragment your focus.
- At the end of the day, you know you were busy, but question what you got done.

- As a result, work comes at the expense of your personal life, sacrificing the things that matter most: family, health, and well-being.

> **For the first time in history, there is a way to make faster, smarter decisions without any of the sacrifice: by harnessing artificial intelligence as your strategic Thought Partner.**

If you're in this boat, take heart. Most leaders are right there with you. But even if you're managing to stay afloat and carving out time for strategic thinking, you're still running into other major barriers:

- You find yourself waiting for your data team's insights. You're stuck in line with all the other competing demands. This means decisions often get delayed, or they're made with incomplete or outdated information.
- The wealth of data paradoxically leads to decision-making paralysis. You struggle to sift through the noise for genuine insights. As a result, you can easily steer your strategy in the wrong direction.

Strategic thinking is nonnegotiable for your business. It requires deliberate, uninterrupted time to reflect on long-term opportunities. Up until recently, it required a ton of time to properly sift through all the data. In the past, you would have to get off-site to unplug for days at a time to do this thinking. It was important work, but very time-consuming and disruptive. There wasn't really an ideal solution.

But now, the game has changed. For the first time in history, there is a way to make faster, smarter decisions without any of the sacrifice: *by harnessing artificial intelligence as your strategic Thought Partner.*

A New Category of Leader: The AI-Driven Leader

***By the way, I've taken the liberty to underline insights I believe will bring you the most value. Enjoy!**

What if you could make brilliant decisions in *minutes* rather than months or years? What if you could be more like Netflix and less like Blockbuster? You can, with AI as your Thought Partner. The true game changer isn't using AI to craft better emails; it's harnessing AI to elevate your strategic thinking.

The first step to becoming an AI-driven leader is changing your limiting beliefs around AI. You need to believe that AI will enhance you, not replace you. Rather than seeing AI as a threat (or a cheap parlor trick), recognize that it's a powerful ally in making faster, smarter decisions. One that shifts you from operational overwhelm to strategic clarity, helping you build a better business and better lives.

The second step is shifting your behavior. **Instead of asking, "How can I do this?" start asking, "How can AI help me do this?"** Here are three big problems AI can help you solve immediately.

1. Turning Data into Decisions

In your business, the issue isn't a lack of information but an overwhelming flood of it. To compound the problem, every leader has biases and assumptions that can distort judgment, leading to strategic missteps. These biases often go unnoticed, but they influence decision-making, sometimes in damaging ways. Author Keith

Cunningham speaks of losing over $100 million in his own ventures due to unchecked assumptions and overly optimistic thinking. As Keith said, "Nothing is worse than running enthusiastically in the wrong direction."

Finding a way to filter out the noise, mute your biases, and pinpoint what's relevant is key. This is where AI becomes invaluable. Simply asking AI to challenge your biases or identify new growth strategies can yield fresh perspectives, drive diverse decision-making, and improve overall strategy. Want to experience how AI can enhance your thinking? Try this prompt:

> Attached is our strategic plan. I want you to act as my AI Thought Partner™ by asking me one question at a time to challenge my biases and the assumptions we have made. I also want you to challenge if our plan has the sufficiency to achieve our goal. Once you have enough information, give me a summary of where you think our plan is strong and where you see potential weaknesses, and recommend ways we can improve it.

You don't have to drown yourself in data and feel overwhelmed when making decisions. Let AI do the heavy lifting by analyzing huge volumes of data to reveal patterns and serve up relevant insights in seconds. As an AI-driven leader, you can merge the best of your instincts with AI's processing power. By blending technology with humanity, you ensure your decisions are not only data-driven but also grounded in critical thinking. AI doesn't replace what makes you human; it enhances it, helping you turn data into actionable decisions that drive your business forward.

2. Doing More with Less

AI enables you to achieve more with fewer resources. You can automate routine tasks and streamline processes. This means reallocating your team's efforts from mundane activities to high-impact priorities that drive business value and supercharging them with AI. You'll move from feeling stressed and pressured to achieving more with less.

Boston Consulting Group conducted a study with Harvard to evaluate what impact AI might have on 758 of their consultants. The study showed that those who used AI had a 40% increase in the quality of their work. They completed tasks 25% faster and were able to tackle 12.2% more tasks than those without AI.

3. Aligning Short-Term Efforts With Long-Term Vision

As leaders, we are not strangers to the immense pressure to deliver fast results. Delivering in the short term is important, but the pressure can skew our focus, causing us to sacrifice the long-term priorities that sustain growth.

The challenge lies not only in the pressure to produce quick wins but also in the natural tendency of organizations to reward short-term performance. This creates a culture where decisions are made with a narrow focus, potentially compromising your long-term competitive advantage.

Turn to AI as your Thought Partner here, conducting virtual interviews to align your short-term efforts with your long-term vision. Scenario planning helps you anticipate future challenges and balance immediate wins with strategic goals. By harnessing AI as your Thought Partner, you can ensure you hit short-term goals while making progress on the initiatives that drive long-term growth. It's simply a matter of asking the right questions.

Why You Can't Afford to Wait Any Longer

According to Eric Schmidt, the former CEO of Google, with the pace at which AI is evolving, it is entirely reasonable to expect we will be living in a fundamentally different world within the next five years. Not ten. Five.

If you've hesitated on embracing AI, consider this your wake-up call. I'm not going to tell you that if you don't adopt AI, you'll be put out of business. That's just hype. What I will say is that your job as a leader is to prepare your company to withstand a variety of future conditions and continue to grow in spite of them.

The writing is on the wall: the world is becoming AI-driven. If you want your company to thrive, let alone survive, you need to understand what AI is and how you can harness it to build a competitive advantage. This is not something you can wait any longer on because there is a learning curve, and this is not something you can delegate to someone on your team. Getting educated is your job. You need to start now.

By harnessing AI as your strategic Thought Partner, you can build a competitive advantage. If you do not, you risk your competitors beating you to it. The goal of this book is to transform you into an AI-driven leader. One who's able to finally get out of the day-to-day grind and lead with strategic clarity so you can make faster, smarter decisions and accelerate the growth of your organization.

I believe with the right leadership, you can create a world where the majority of your people's time is invested in high-impact priorities, aligned with their strengths, supercharged by AI. This will lead to disruptive results without disrupting your organization. By embracing your position within this new category of leader, you place yourself among forward-thinking pioneers who are shaping the future of leadership itself. You're not just keeping up with technology; you're defining a new standard for how to harness it. Join us. This is a meaningful journey we get to embark on together.

What You Will Learn in This Book

This book is written for innovative executives, strategically minded leaders, and impact-driven visionaries. You will get the most out of this book by using it as a guide to accelerate the growth of your business, gain a competitive advantage, and create better lives for your people.

To help you do this, I've structured the book in three main parts:

1. Part 1 redefines your leadership in the AI era
2. Part 2 helps you become an AI-driven leader
3. Part 3 helps you build an AI-driven organization

In the following chapters, we'll explore the skills and lessons you need to become an effective AI-driven leader. You'll discover how to transition from operational overwhelm to leading with strategic clarity. Here's an overview of what's to come:

Ch. 1	The rise of AI and the AI-Driven Leader (you're reading this now)
Ch. 2	Lessons from past technological disruptions that you can apply to your leadership today
Ch. 3	Mindset shifts that will help your team embrace AI instead of resist it
Ch. 4	Understand what AI is, how it works, and how to get started
Ch. 5	Five simple use cases you can apply today to supercharge your leadership
Ch. 6	The high price of asking the wrong questions and how you can use AI to overcome your biases and assumptions
Ch. 7	How to turn data into decisions, collapsing what used to take weeks into minutes
Ch. 8	How to use AI to navigate short-term pressures without sacrificing long-term growth

Ch. 9	A proven framework to make faster, smarter decisions
Ch. 10	How to lead with strategic clarity to alignment all year long
Ch. 11	How to win the first 30 days and turn your strategic plan into results
Ch. 12	How to 10x the impact of every employee in your organization
Ch. 13	Change management strategies to ensure you integrate AI seamlessly into your organization
Ch. 14	Simple steps to go from 0 to 1 with AI, delivering immediate value

Throughout the book, I'll share stories to keep things entertaining. You'll also get real use cases showing how leaders are harnessing AI to make faster, smarter decisions. Company names will be shared when possible, but sometimes, for confidentiality, they will be changed or omitted. For example, you'll learn how one company collapsed hundreds of hours of work into minutes using the right prompt. You'll discover how one executive team leveraged AI to smooth out interactions with an activist board. And you'll see how a leader reduced six months of client work into two weeks, leaving his competitors flat-footed.

I'll share many of my most valuable prompts that you can use immediately to get quick wins. You can also find every prompt in the appendix section of the book. Additionally, I've developed an AI Thought Partner™ trained on this book's content to provide you with personalized guidance throughout. This innovative tool allows you to interact with the book's content and prompts in real time, ask specific questions, and receive tailored advice. My hope is that this helps you apply what you learn here by enhancing your strategic thinking and decision-making. Just visit AiLeadership.com or scan the QR code when presented.

Your Greatest Strengths. Amplified.

Scan the QR code to discover how AI can turn your strengths into superpowers and multiply your impact where it matters most.

Finally, I'll show you how to transform your team from task masters into innovative, strategic thinkers. We will present a new way for your team to prioritize their time and discuss how to integrate AI into the way you work to drive growth. By the end of this book, you'll have the mindset, skills, and tools to thrive as an AI-driven leader.

What You Will Not Get from This Book

If you're comfortable with the status quo or waiting for someone else to figure out AI at some future date, this book is not for you. This is for ambitious, innovative, growth-minded leaders who are unsatisfied with the status quo, are committed to building a better business and better lives for their people, and see AI as a catalyst for that growth. If that is you, then you've found your tribe.

This book is also not about AI because tech adoption is not your goal. AI is simply a tool to help you achieve your goals. Throughout this book, you will notice a recurring theme: **strategy first; technology second. While AI is a timely tool, strategy is**

timeless. That's why this is not an AI book; it's a leadership book. Your leadership is what will make the difference.

I will focus on equipping you with timeless strategic skills that will help you thrive in any technological era and then show you how to enhance them with AI. While doing this, I will intentionally steer clear of specific AI tools or governance policies because the technology evolves so rapidly that today's hot platform could become irrelevant tomorrow. For personalized guidance on choosing the right AI tools for your business, visit AiLeadership.com. Discover my latest recommendations and engage with our AI Thought Partner™ trained on this book's content. I encourage you to ask it questions so it can help you take your first steps in applying what you learn to get results.

My Path to Becoming an AI-Driven Leader

My first introduction to strategic thinking was in my senior year of college. I was interning at a startup technology company, and I asked the CEO what job I should get after graduation. His answer surprised me, "Geoff, you're asking the wrong question! You should be asking, **'What are the skills I can master that are so valuable they will serve me no matter where I go? And what jobs can help me develop those skills?'"**

This is the first time I realize the power of asking the right questions. It's also the best career advice I've ever received.

Fast forward seven years. I was working in medical device sales, running through hospitals each day, selling devices that made a positive impact on patients. My career was going well, but I was unfulfilled. Growth was my number-one core value, yet every day I felt like I was meant for more and playing below my potential. It was downright painful.

Then one day, I heard a speech that changed my life. I was in attendance at our national sales meeting when a man named Jay Papasan stepped on stage. Over the next hour, he delivered a keynote about a concept called *The ONE Thing*. It was based on the bestselling book he co-wrote with Gary Keller, the founder of Keller Williams, the largest real estate company in the world by agent count. The idea was simple but incredibly powerful: identify the one thing you could do such that by doing it, everything else would be easier or unnecessary.

Jay finished his speech and got a standing ovation. When the crowd finally sat down, I found myself still standing. My mind was telling me to sit, but my heart was telling me to run to the stage to talk with Jay. I listened to my heart and was suddenly running down the side of the ballroom so I could be the first person to talk to Jay. I had no idea this conversation would change my life.

Jay and I developed a relationship. Eventually he told me that *The ONE Thing* created a unique challenge. On the one hand, it was a massive hit and was one of the highest-rated business books. The problem was, Gary's ONE thing was being chairman of Keller Williams. Jay's ONE thing was writing books with Gary. They were missing someone whose ONE thing could be *The ONE Thing*. That became my opportunity.

On November 1, 2015, I moved my family from Southern California to Austin, Texas, to partner with Gary and Jay to turn their book into a comprehensive training and consulting company.

My first ninety days were defined by a steep challenge: cast a compelling vision for the business and generate $100,000 in revenue out of thin air, or I would be fired. Needless to say, I felt immense pressure to deliver results. For the next ninety days, I worked extremely hard and got the job done. But I was about to find out that there was now a much bigger problem.

I will always remember walking into the boardroom to present the results of my first ninety days. Inflated with pride and expecting praise,

I announced that we had hit our revenue goals. But Gary looked me in the eyes and said, "Geoff, your product sucks!"

I was floored. How could this be true? Customers were giving great reviews, and we had zero refunds. How could our product suck?

He then looked at me and asked, "How many customers did your customers bring you?"

I looked at him and realized the problem. I admitted defeat. *None*.

He leaned in and said, "You'll know you have a world-class product when every customer brings you another customer. Go build that!"

That lesson stuck with me. Later, it would shape 'remarkable experiences' as a core value of AI Leadership—everything we do should be so remarkable that people actually remark about it.

During my tenure at The ONE Thing, I also coached Naveen Jindal, the chairman of Jindal Steel & Power, and his executive team. JSP is a global steel powerhouse out of India. After seven years of building the company behind The ONE Thing, it was time for a new chapter in my career. I exited the company and sold my shares back to Gary and Jay. Shortly after I left the company, Mr. Jindal called me and asked if I would come in-house.

I said, "It depends. What's the job?"

He replied, "You know our business. You tell me."

I stepped in as global chief growth officer, responsible for working alongside the Jindal family to drive growth across all our portfolio companies, including India, the Middle East, Africa, and Australia. **While I was working at JSP, with the strong leadership of the Jindals and our talented executives, the company's market cap grew from $750 million to $12 billion.**

It was on one of my quarterly trips to India that I first discovered AI. When I saw it, it stopped me in my tracks. I wanted to take action, but then I thought, 'I'm so busy, I'll get to this later or delegate it to someone on the technical team.' But then, a question from my senior year of college began echoing in my mind:

"What are the skills I can master that are so valuable they will serve me no matter where I go?"

I set a goal to master AI to increase my impact in the Jindal Group. The more I began to understand it, the more confident I was that this was the future. Eventually, I had a conversation with Mr. Jindal where I said just that: "This is the future. As chairman, you need to own this at the board level so we can drive it through all of our companies."

He looked at me and asked, "Why don't you do it for me?"

Game on! The challenge was, I didn't know how. This is when I remembered something I learned from Gary Keller, "Anytime you're hitting a ceiling of achievement, you're just missing a person." For me, that person was Google, and together, we formed a partnership.

Every quarter, when I was in Delhi, I was at their headquarters. They taught me what the technology was, how it worked, and how to identify the right use cases. But as we started driving AI adoption in the company, I saw something no one was talking about—the gap between AI as a tool and AI as a leadership advantage.

At the time, tech companies and consultants were selling AI as a magic bullet—a solution in search of a problem. But no one was addressing the real driver of success: you—the leader. The companies making the biggest gains weren't just implementing AI. They had leaders who knew how to wield it. The real question wasn't just about AI—it was about who you could become to leverage it and win in an AI-driven future.

That realization changed everything. It drove me to resign from Jindal Steel, write this book, and build AI Leadership—a strategic advisory company that installs AI-driven execution systems to turn your strategy into financial value in a fraction of the time.

What if your job wasn't to become an AI expert? What if your job was to become an AI-driven leader?

Meaning, you use the technology every day so you can cast a vision for the future, define your strategy to win, and lead the change—while ensuring AI enhances your people rather than replaces them.

As you become an AI-driven leader, you might think the challenge is keeping up with AI. It's not.

The real problem is that your organization was never designed to move at the speed AI requires to win.

Most leadership teams are moving too slow. Think about how long it takes to clarify your strategy. To align your teams. To make decisions. To adjust when priorities shift.

Months.

While you're debating, AI is transforming the landscape around you.

By the time your plan is finalized, it's already outdated. And every time priorities shift, the effort required to realign the organization slows you down even more.

So what happens?

There's a lot of activity—but not a lot of results. AI only amplifies this.

Becoming an AI-driven leader isn't about chasing use cases or becoming an expert in the technology. It's about transforming how you think, how you lead, and how your organization executes—because in an AI-driven world, speed is now your advantage, and execution determines if you win.

What if there was a way to harness AI to create faster clarity, tighter alignment, better decisions, and a system that keeps your strategy current as everything around you changes—so you can actually capture the full value AI makes possible?

That's the work we now do with companies—installing an AI-driven strategy execution system that fundamentally changes how leadership teams operate. We work alongside you to align faster, execute better, and continuously adapt so you move at the speed required to win.

The Big Idea in AI-Driven Leadership

What if the biggest threat to your business is not your competition, but your own thinking?

Right now, AI isn't just changing how we work—it's reshaping how we think. Most people use generative AI in one of two ways: as a smarter Google to answer questions or as an assistant to help with tasks like writing better emails. While both can be useful, they barely scratch the surface of what's possible.

You have an opportunity to raise your standards for your relationship with this technology. Instead of using AI for the 80% of tasks that drive only 20% of your results, harness it for the 20% of priorities that drive 80% of your success. As a leader, that is your ability to think strategically and make faster, smarter decisions.

This requires a shift in perspective. You are the Thought Leader—AI is your Thought Partner. Instead of just asking AI questions, turn the tables and have it ask you the right questions. When used this way, you can solve your most complicated problems and achieve your most ambitious goals.

This book is your guide to making that shift. But more than that, it's an invitation to step into a movement—one that will define the future of leadership.

Together, we are creating a new category of leader: The AI-Driven Leader—one who harnesses AI to build better businesses and better lives.

Every technological shift in history has created a divide between those who adapt and those who hesitate. AI is no different. The leaders already using AI as their Thought Partner are gaining an edge, compounding their advantage over time. Those waiting for clarity are falling behind.

In the next chapter, we'll look at what past technological revolutions can teach you about navigating these shifts without chaos. Because if history has proven anything, it's that the leaders who understand the pattern of disruption don't just survive change—they shape it.

> **"Together, we are creating a new category of leader: The AI-Driven Leader—one who harnesses AI to build better businesses and better lives."**

CHAPTER 2

We've Been Here Before: What Past Technological Revolutions Can Teach AI-Driven Leaders

John D. Rockefeller was the founder of Standard Oil and once the wealthiest man on Earth. In the early twentieth century, he recognized a problem. The US was in the middle of a massive transformation, shifting from agriculture to industry, with booming sectors like oil and steel driving the change.

The surge in factories created a demand for a new type of worker: the industrial worker. However, there was a catch. The education system was prioritizing teaching kids critical thinking and independent inquiry—skills that didn't align with the needs of the Industrial Era.

Rockefeller saw an opportunity to shape the future workforce. Rumored to have said, "I don't want a nation of thinkers. I want a nation of workers," Rockefeller envisioned a new workforce that would arrive on time, follow orders, and perform repetitive tasks quickly and efficiently. In this new way of working, skills like strategic thinking, creativity, problem-solving, communication, and collaboration took a back seat to the demands of the industrial machine.

To address this misalignment, Rockefeller established the General Education Board in 1902, pouring in $1 million (equivalent to $37 million today). With guidance from Rockefeller's advisor, Frederick T. Gates, the Board set out to reshape American public education, aiming to create industrial workers instead of nurturing thinkers.

Over the decades, the Board invested over $100 million, emphasizing rote learning, punctuality, and obedience. While this model aligned perfectly with industrialists' need for a compliant workforce, it sidelined many of our human strengths in the process of adapting to working with machines.

The impact of Rockefeller's influence on the public education system is still evident in today's classrooms. Students are trained to show up on time, listen to lectures, and memorize facts, and they get rewarded for correct answers. This task-focused mentality carries over into the workplace, where employees often defer to leaders for direction, set safe goals, and look to their superiors for answers instead of thinking strategically.

As a result, leaders find themselves managing people who are focused on task completion, processes, and punctuality. This limits the growth of strategic and creative skills. It also stunts development and creates a shortage of internal candidates for leadership roles, reinforcing a cycle of operational thinking.

As we become AI-driven leaders, it's time to break free from this cycle and shift our focus from operational to strategic thinking. Our humanity lies in our ability to think strategically, be creative, and communicate and collaborate to solve complex problems. The Industrial Revolution required setting aside these strengths to meet the needs of machinery. AI presents a unique opportunity to reclaim them and have machines adjust to meet our needs. It's important to understand that while AI will require you to change, it will not replace you; instead, it will enhance you.

Rick Heitzmann, Managing Director of FirstMark Capital, agrees. He told me, "This is going to be an incredible tool for knowledge workers. The people who can adopt it will become a lot more efficient and gain a competitive advantage."

AI-driven leaders see this shift as an opportunity to do more with less, focusing on high-impact priorities aligned with their unique human strengths, while technology handles low-value tasks. According to McKinsey, 50% of the activities people are paid to do could be automated with existing technology. While this may seem daunting, I believe this shift will be net positive for us. Throughout history, each technological change has brought some risk and downside, but overall, our quality of life has improved. I believe the same will hold true with AI. Yes, some jobs will be eliminated and privacy and security risks remain, but the positives of AI are immense.

Take advantage of this opportunity. As an AI-driven leader, you can free yourself from the operational weeds, giving you time for strategic

"AI won't replace you; those who harness AI will replace those who don't."

thinking, creativity, problem-solving, communication, and collaboration. This will help you build a better business and better lives for your people. Unlike in the past, you now have the opportunity to have machines adjust to meet your needs and amplify your strengths.

This brings us to a crucial point: It's essential to identify which skills are so valuable that mastering them will serve you no matter where you go. AI won't replace you; those who harness AI will replace those who don't. The choice is clear: learn the skill of harnessing AI ethically to build an advantage, or cling to outdated ways of working and risk being left behind.

These choices aren't new—the technology is. We've faced similar disruptions before, and Nokia's story serves as a cautionary tale of what happens when companies fail to adapt to technological change.

From Dominance to Downfall: How Nokia's Story Guides AI-Driven Leaders

At its peak, Nokia controlled a staggering 49% share of the mobile phone market. However, the company's inability to adapt to swift technological changes ultimately led to their downfall, serving as a cautionary tale for leaders in the AI era.

Nokia's inability to adapt and innovate proved to be a critical misstep. The leadership team, having dominated the mobile phone space with their hardware expertise, underestimated the smartphone revolution and was slow to pivot. They failed to recognize that mastering smartphones required a solid grasp of both hardware and software. Instead of questioning their biases and assumptions, Nokia's leaders became complacent, assuming that past triumphs would guarantee future success. As a result, they missed the opportunity to maintain their competitive advantage in the smartphone market.

Another critical error compounded their problems: Nokia's flawed marketing strategy. Leadership assumed their product would speak for itself, a strategy that had worked in the past. However, when Apple launched the iPhone 2G, it put substantial marketing muscle behind each of its fifteen technical improvements, making each feature seem like a groundbreaking innovation. But here's the thing: Nokia's flagship N95, which came out before the iPhone 2G, had fourteen of those fifteen features, plus many extras that the iPhone lacked. The problem? No one knew! The difference-maker wasn't the product itself but the strategic thinking and decisions of the leadership team. Steve Jobs recognized that strategy meant building an advantage in the long term through the actions taken in the short term. He crafted compelling stories as if Apple's future depended on it—and it worked!

Reflecting on my own journey, when I first launched AI Leadership, I shared my vision with a friend, Jayme Hoffman. He posed a question that he'd once been asked in the renowned tech incubator Y Combinator: "Geoff, how many potential customers have you spoken to who said they want to buy what you're selling?" My answer was zero! Jayme challenged me to speak with 100 potential customers and then revisit my vision.

In my initial plan, I'd assumed three things:

1. Leaders believe AI is the future
2. Leaders believe their business will adopt AI
3. Leaders are actively pursuing AI adoption

But after conducting over 200 one-on-one interviews with executives, I was stunned by my findings:

1. 100% of them said they believe AI is the future
2. 100% of them believed their businesses would adopt AI
3. Less than 5% had done anything because they didn't know where to start and feared they were falling behind.

This disconnect became the driving force behind this book. Through my interviews, I discovered that while executives acknowledge the need to adopt AI "eventually," three main obstacles held them back:

1. They were too busy with all the existing demands of the business.
2. They didn't understand what AI was or how it could help them.
3. No one had showed them the simple path to go from 0 to 1 with AI in a way that would create value for them.

I realized the simple path to go from 0 to 1 with AI wasn't weaving it into products or services or boosting operational efficiency. It was putting AI in the hands of leaders so they could experience its incredible value firsthand. Once a leader believes in AI's potential, then they can drive it through their company. This would not come from showing them how to write a better email. That is not what drives business value. But enhancing their strategic thinking and decision-making? Now, that's a game changer!

Strategic thinking and decision-making have always been critical leadership skills. However, our education system often grades you on your ability to have the answer, not on your ability to search for one. The problem is, this approach falls short in the business world, where you are faced with a multitude of puzzle pieces without a clear picture to reference. Great strategic thinkers are masters of asking questions they don't yet have the answer to and searching for those answers. Developing this skill on your own requires practice, but AI can collapse the learning curve.

Imagine a time you were standing at a whiteboard with a Thought Partner. You shared an idea, and they immediately started to build on it. Before you knew it, you were engaged in a fast-paced, back-and-forth dialogue where it seemed like one plus one could equal eleven. This is the power of engaging AI as your Thought Partner.

To seize this moment, help your people shed old habits of waiting for direction and focusing solely on task completion. Train them to think strategically. Guide them in using AI as a Thought Partner, and show them how to deliver greater results in less time.

While this is an exciting opportunity, it's important to acknowledge your people's fears and worries. Many are concerned about losing their jobs, while others worry about the broader impact AI might have on humanity. Their fears are legitimate. The difference between AI's impact being net positive or negative lies not in the technology itself but in the leaders using it. In this way, history is repeating itself.

> **"Strategic thinking and decision-making have always been critical leadership skills. However, our education system often grades you on your ability to have the answer, not on your ability to search for one."**

Turning Points in Tech History

Throughout history, technological disruptions have transformed societies, workplaces, and leadership. By analyzing the influence of the printing press, the assembly line, and the internet, you can learn vital lessons as an AI-driven leader navigating today's technological shifts.

The Printing Press

Before the printing press, knowledge was reserved for society's elite—clergy, royalty, wealthy landowners, and scholars. Ordinary people, who couldn't read or write and lacked access to books, relied on oral traditions and their immediate environment for education. This knowledge gap stunted personal and societal progress.

The printing press, invented by Johannes Gutenberg in the mid-fifteenth century, revolutionized the production of books through its use of movable type. This innovation dramatically reduced the time and cost required to produce books and allowed for their mass production. While the press democratized information, it also sparked both awe and fear. Scribes worried about losing their jobs, and those who wielded power, like the Church, feared the loss of control. Pope Alexander VI himself wrote, "It will be necessary to maintain full control over the printers so that they may be prevented from bringing into print writings which are antagonistic to the Catholic faith, or which are likely to cause trouble to believers."

Despite some of these fears coming to pass, the printing press prevailed, opening up an era of unprecedented information access. As books became more widespread and affordable, literacy rates soared, fueling intellectual progress during the Scientific Revolution and Enlightenment. The technology also spurred religious and social upheaval, enabling the spread of ideas that challenged the status quo.

Beyond ideas, the printing press shaped economic and social landscapes. Cities that quickly adopted the technology became centers of learning, commerce, and prosperity. Those that lagged behind missed the wave. The printing press was a big step forward for humanity.

The Assembly Line

Before the assembly line, manufacturing was dominated by skilled artisans. Blacksmiths and carpenters transformed raw materials into finished products from start to finish. There was a tremendous sense of pride and ownership that came with craftsmanship. However, it was time-consuming and costly, and it limited the quantity that could be produced and sold.

The assembly line created a seismic shift in production. Suddenly, products moved sequentially from one workstation to the next. Each worker would perform a specific task on the item before passing it down the line to the next station. Efficiency soared while the time to produce a single item collapsed. Business was booming! But it also brought fears of job loss and concern that the value of human work would be reduced with the shift from craftsmanship to the monotony of repetitive tasks. Many of these fears came true. The shift did reduce the demand for handmade products in favor of more affordable options. This meant the value of craftsmanship skills declined, and the value of industrial skills increased, requiring workers to conform to the machine and set aside their human strengths. Many craftsmen lost their jobs, while the overall number of jobs available skyrocketed. They simply required different skills.

One major result of assembly line production was the widespread availability of affordable cars, which significantly impacted the American way of life. It gave people the freedom to live farther from work, spurring the growth of suburban communities. With cars, families had the freedom to travel for leisure. Economically, new industries boomed, such as oil, rubber, and road construction. This created more jobs and fueled economic growth. There were downsides to the new technology, but the assembly line enabled humanity to take a big step forward.

The Internet

The internet went mainstream by the late 1990s, reshaping how we communicate, work, and live. Imagine a world where business required face-to-face meetings and letters took days to deliver. Shopping, banking, and communication all demanded your physical presence. Life moved at a slower pace, with information trickling through traditional channels. This was life before the internet.

The technology was a game changer that revolutionized our lives. Suddenly, communicating with someone halfway across the globe became instant and virtually free. Information was no longer a scarce resource but a flood, accessible at our fingertips. The internet powered economic growth, adding $2.45 trillion to the US GDP in 2020 and creating over seventeen million jobs. It transformed work, with software automating routine tasks and shifting the demand to skills like creativity, problem-solving, and digital fluency. Remote work, once a novelty, became more common post-COVID-19, offering flexibility and a better work-life balance.

However, like all previous technological disruptions, the internet sparked both excitement and fear. Like with the printing press and assembly line, certain skills and processes became outdated. This was relevant for traditional industries like print media, postal services, and travel agencies, which all faced massive disruptions, causing people to lose jobs.

The internet also had material downsides for us as humans. Despite being more connected than ever, we are also more disconnected. Think about the couple on a date, engaging with their phones instead of each other. Social media has been linked to an epidemic of teen depression and anxiety. The cybersecurity industry has boomed, with spending hitting $71.1 billion in 2022. Elections have been targeted by misinformation campaigns, with social media spreading false information that makes it tough to separate fact from fiction.

The internet has been a net positive for humanity, but it also provides a tough lesson about what happens when leaders focus only on profits and ignore human well-being. Sure, driving shareholder value is part of the job, but it can't be the only focus. With social media, leaders missed the bigger picture. We have allowed platforms to exploit our weaknesses through addictive design and algorithms that promote harmful content, spread hate, and reinforce biases. All this to the detriment of you, me, and our children—for profit.

Between 2017 and 2024, Congress held forty hearings on social media and its impact on our children. Guess how many laws have been passed. Zero! This highlights the lack of meaningful action despite clear evidence of harm.

Here's why this matters to you. We have a responsibility to think about the long-term impact on society. Real leadership means balancing profit with a commitment to moving humanity forward in a positive way.

This is a wake-up call for you as an AI-driven leader. AI is just a tool, it is not inherently good or bad. Its impact depends on how you harness it. As you navigate AI adoption, you have a choice: repeat past mistakes by prioritizing short-term gains at the expense of long-term sustainability, or hold yourself to a higher standard. The definition of insanity is doing the same thing over and over and expecting different results. Let's learn from our past and commit to using AI as a tool to build better businesses and better lives.

I want to be clear. While AI can replace many things, it can't replace the value of human connection and leadership. Technology transforms industries, but human guidance is essential in shaping a future that prioritizes well-being and ethical use.

Each of these past innovations brought significant changes, both opportunities and challenges. As AI is set to be the next disruption, there are valuable lessons you can learn from the past to navigate the future effectively.

Lessons for AI-Driven Leaders

Embrace change. Adapt quickly, and keep people at the center. Leaders who adapted quickly and saw potential in the unknown thrived during past disruptions. While AI raises concerns around job security and safety, with strong leadership, you can navigate these challenges so you can drive your business forward and keep your people's interests at the center.

Become a practice leader. By using AI yourself, you'll build credibility and trust because you're on the journey with them. This book will show you how.

Communicate effectively and transparently. There are many benefits you will gain by adopting AI, and if history repeats itself, there will also be some downsides. The key difference lies not in the technology but in your leadership.

Strong leadership will present a balance of optimism for the benefits that will come while also being transparent about the risks, so you'll gain trust as you lead your team ethically and transparently through the change.

On the positives, it is important that you communicate a compelling vision for why you believe this change will be a net positive for the business and people overall. This will help people find the motivation to go through the change.

It is also important that you be transparent about the risks and what you do not yet know. Many of your people fear losing their jobs. Empathize and help them understand that their jobs are simply combinations of skills applied and processes followed. It is true that certain skills and processes will be taken over by AI, but AI will not replace *them* as humans. There will be a demand for new skills and processes, and that is something they can learn!

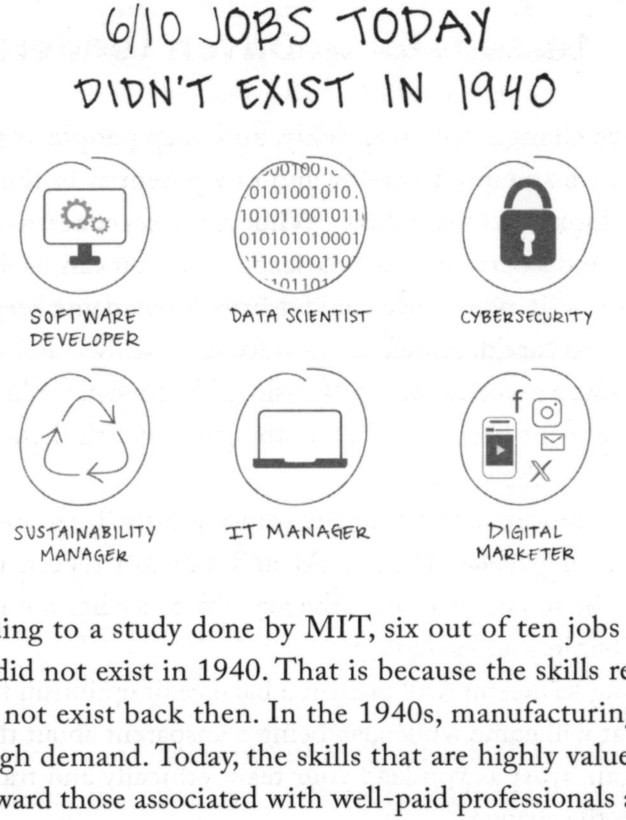

According to a study done by MIT, six out of ten jobs people do today did not exist in 1940. That is because the skills required today did not exist back then. In the 1940s, manufacturing skills were in high demand. Today, the skills that are highly valued have shifted toward those associated with well-paid professionals and service-based work.

What you do today may not be what you do tomorrow. Skills and processes change over time, but this doesn't mean you will lose your job. It means your role might evolve, either within the same company or in a different one. This shift doesn't replace you as a human; it transforms how you work from the old way to the new way. View this as an opportunity to advance your career, develop valuable skills, and find more fulfillment. Resist, and you may struggle with the transition and risk losing your competitive edge.

Lead with empathetic strength. As an AI-driven leader, your job isn't to ensure your people's happiness or eliminate their fear. It's to build the best business possible in an ethical manner, keeping your people's interests at the center. **I call this leading with empathetic strength.** This means balancing the space for your people's fears and concerns with the strength to make decisions in the best interest of the business.

You have an obligation to consider implementing AI. How you choose to adopt it is up to you. Additionally, you have a responsibility to help your people grow their skills in your company as you become AI-driven. This allows them to stay current and continue making an impact. Whether they choose to evolve their skills is up to them.

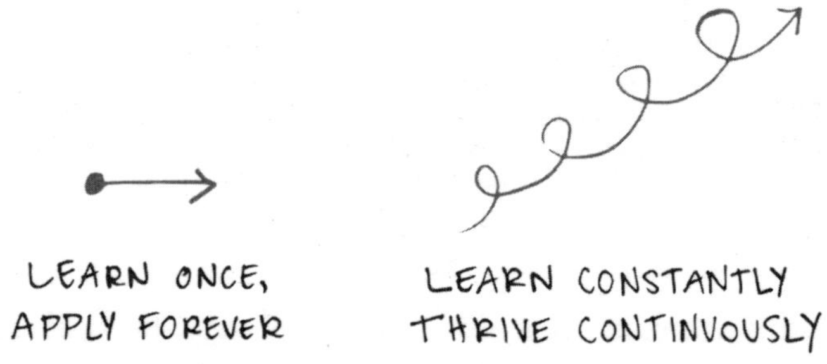

Develop skills for the future. We are shifting from industrial skills to AI-driven skills. This means reclaiming our human strengths of creativity, strategic thinking, problem-solving, communication, and collaboration. It is also a shift from the industrial mindset of "learn once, apply forever" to an AI-driven mindset of "learn constantly, thrive continuously."

Empower your people to shape the future. Authorship is ownership. When you involve your people in building the future, they feel a sense of ownership. Inviting their ideas and insights as you adopt

AI will empower them to develop new skills. It will also build trust as a shared vision for the future emerges.

History has shown that every technological disruption reshapes the value of human skills. AI is no different. It has the potential to enhance productivity, streamline operations, and revolutionize customer experiences. But technology alone isn't the differentiator—leadership is. The leaders who surround themselves with the right people, challenge their own thinking, and continuously learn will be the ones who define the future.

And defining the future requires clarity on your role.

As you develop your relationship with AI, you must acknowledge that one of you will play the "Thought Leader" role and the other the "Thought Partner—and that distinction makes all the difference."

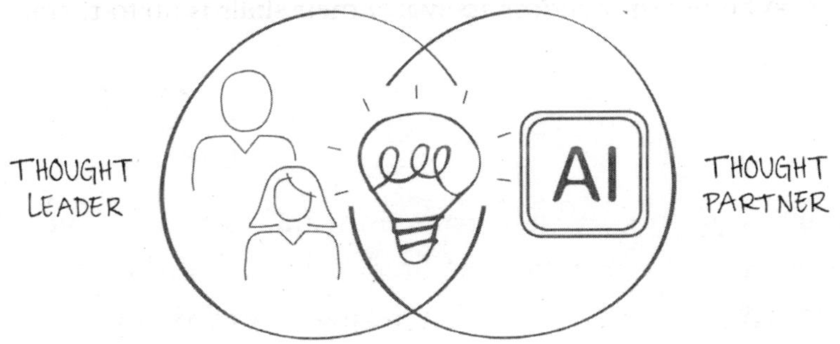

Your Role as the Thought Leader

As the Thought Leader, your role is to direct AI where to focus and what to do so it can do the heavy lifting. This is not a new skill. You do this when you leverage the people on your team to get work done. As the Thought Leader, you communicate the direction and let the team come up with the plan and own the execution to deliver the result. It will be the same with AI as a new strategic partner on your team. The important thing to remember is that AI lacks the context and perspective you bring to the table. It lacks your leadership. This is why you must remain in the role of Thought Leader.

As your Thought Partner, AI can help clarify your thinking, enhance your decisions, structure communication, analyze data, challenge your biases, and narrow your focus. It is a powerful tool if you know how to harness it correctly.

This partnership allows you to shift from operational overwhelm to strategic clarity, a mindset shift that is essential for leaders in the AI-driven world.

By establishing this relationship—where you are the Thought Leader and AI your Thought Partner—you can make better decisions, solve problems more effectively, and drive accelerated growth. Embrace this new partnership. It can help you achieve things you previously thought were impossible. It certainly has for me.

In the next chapter, we will explore the mindset shift required to fully embrace this new role and unlock the potential of AI-driven leadership.

"Change may be uncomfortable, but it's where growth happens."

Here's the 20% from This Chapter that Delivers 80% of the Value

1. **Embrace Change:** Change may be uncomfortable, but it's where growth happens. Treat it as an opportunity to build better businesses and lives.
2. **Become a Practice Leader:** AI adoption starts with you. As a practice leader, you'll share the benefits you've gained and the risks you're navigating.
3. **Communicate Transparently:** Cast a vision for the future. Share how you've benefited, and explain "what's in it for others" when they embrace AI. Empathize with fears and concerns. Be transparent about what you know and what you don't know. Commit to evolving with people's interests at the center.
4. **Invest in Future Skills:** Help your team master valuable skills that will serve them wherever they go. Learning together builds momentum and keeps everyone ahead of the curve.
5. **Empower People to Shape the Future:** Authorship is ownership. Give your people a role in building the future. Leaders who co-create the future with others move further, faster.
6. **Shift from Operational to Strategic:** Use AI on the 20% priorities that matter most.
7. **Prioritize High-Impact Work:** Focus on priorities aligned with human strengths, leaving people fulfilled at the end of the day instead of overwhelmed.

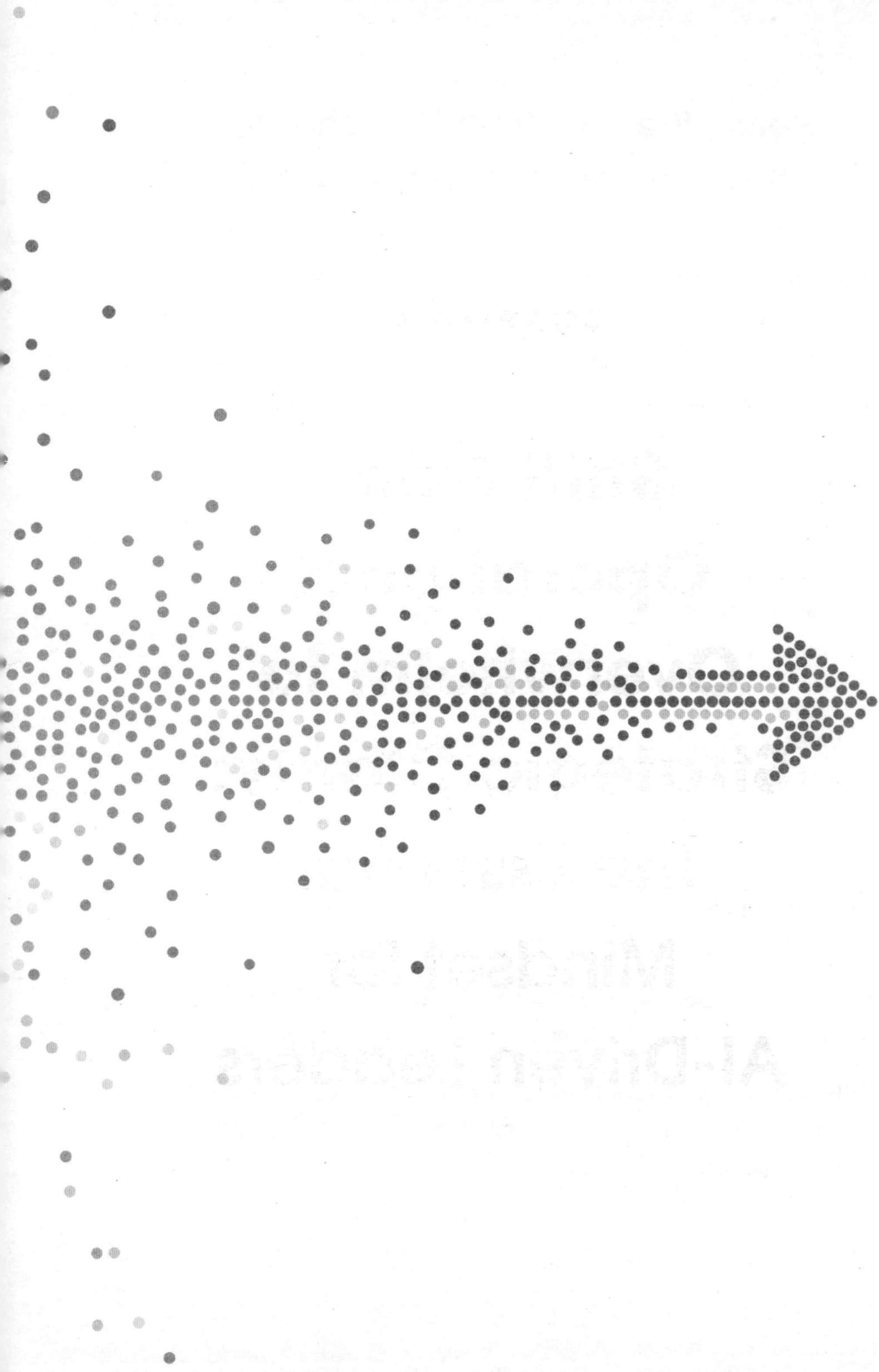

CHAPTER 3

Shift From Operational Overwhelm to Strategic Clarity: The Essential Mindset for AI-Driven Leaders

The year was 2014, and Microsoft, the once leader of the tech industry, now struggled to keep pace with nimble rivals like Google and Apple. As the world shifted to mobile and cloud computing, Microsoft was falling behind, gasping for breath. It was out of touch and slow to adapt.

Enter Satya Nadella.

Stepping in as CEO, Nadella faced a daunting challenge. He saw a company in desperate need of more than a new product or slick marketing campaign—it needed a full-scale transformation to reclaim its competitive edge and claw back to the top.

Nadella believed in the power of a growth mindset, a concept brought to light by psychologist Carol Dweck in her book *Mindset*. People with a growth mindset saw challenges and failures as opportunities to learn, believing that fundamental abilities like intelligence and talent could be developed through effort. By contrast, those with a fixed mindset viewed their traits as set in stone and did not think they could be significantly developed.

When he took over as CEO, Nadella wanted to shift the culture from a bunch of "know-it-alls" to a culture of "learn-it-alls." While this would not be easy, he knew that thinking would drive actions, which would drive results.

Nadella made bold moves: acquiring LinkedIn for a whopping $26 billion, developing the Azure Cloud Platform, and cutting dead weight by streamlining operations and realigning strategic priorities. But perhaps his boldest move was investing in OpenAI, a pioneering AI research firm. Nadella recognized the potential of AI and how it could transform industries. This partnership granted Microsoft access to cutting-edge technology and positioned it as a leader in the AI revolution.

Under Nadella's leadership, Microsoft changed. It regained its competitive edge, became a leader in cloud computing, and saw its market capitalization more than triple. Once again, Microsoft became one of the most valuable and influential tech companies in the world.

Nadella's growth mindset hadn't just turned Microsoft around—it had set it up to thrive in the AI era.

The AI-Driven Leader as a Composer: Casting a Vision and Crafting Strategy

Imagine you are a composer at a grand piano, your eyes closed as you imagine a melody that will hopefully ring throughout concert halls one day. As an AI-driven leader, you are a composer of strategy. You imagine what the future of your organization might look like. You begin to craft a strategic plan that acts as your musical score, outlining the competitive advantage you want to build in the long term. Yet your true genius also lies in clarifying the simple actions your people can take in the short term so they play in harmony to bring your strategy to life.

The AI-Driven Leader as a Conductor of Teams and Technology

As an AI-driven leader, you are also a conductor of teams and technology. You step up to the podium with the orchestra awaiting your direction with instruments in hand. As the conductor, you do not play an instrument yourself; instead, you turn the composer's vision into reality.

This mirrors your role in the business world. With your deep understanding of the vision and the strategic plan, you guide your team to take action. You manage the team dynamics, control the tempo of project execution, and ensure that every section—from marketing to product development—plays in sync. You use technology and artificial intelligence as an instrument, integrating it to enhance the performance of your people so they can create a sound that's greater than the sum of its parts.

The conductor's baton, much like your guidance as a leader, is subtle yet impactful. It might be a gesture that signals the violins or a nod that cues the brass. In your business, it could be a strategic meeting that aligns teams on a new initiative or a technology update that streamlines processes. You ensure that every member of your company understands their role in the concert of business and feels empowered to perform their part to the fullest.

As an AI-driven leader, you embrace the dual role of both composer and conductor. You create strategies that pave the way for competitive advantage and lead the performance of these strategies with the finesse of a maestro. Using the tools and talents at your disposal, you bring your vision to reality. As your business continues to change, it is you as the AI-driven leader who is best equipped to navigate both the challenges and opportunities that lie ahead.

Navigating this transition will require you to evolve your approach to how you interact with your teams. In the industrial way of working, leaders told people what to do, and those people executed. In the world of AI-driven leadership, the value of human work will shift to emphasize our unique human strengths, such as creativity, strategic thinking, problem-solving, communication, and collaboration. If you want different results, you have to demonstrate different leadership behavior. This means shifting from telling people what to do to telling people the vision for the company, your strategic plan to get there, and letting them tell you how they plan to make it happen. That means empowering your people to own their portion of the plan and harness their human strengths, augmented by AI, to make it happen.

This means expecting more thinking leverage from your people. Instead of them waiting for direction, you ask them to bring you their plan in alignment with your goals and strategy. We will cover this in chapter 12.

Why Change Is Hard

Change is the foundation of our evolution—and yet for some reason we *hate* it. Our resistance to change boils down to psychological, organizational, and leadership-related factors.

Psychological Factors

Embracing change is like turning a big ship—it takes time and doesn't happen quickly. We all like things to be predictable and stable because it feels safe. That's why we often stick to old ways of doing things, even when they're not perfect. Changing means stepping into the unknown, which can feel scary.

Fear of the unknown can hold us back. Introducing AI into our work brings uncertainty about our jobs, teams, and ability to keep up. Our brains perceive this big change as a threat, making us reluctant to leave our comfort zone.

Think about a leader who's used to trusting their gut and past experiences to make decisions. Now imagine telling them to use AI for help. It might feel like they're giving up control or that their skills aren't valued as much. This isn't just about learning a new tool—it feels personal.

By understanding these feelings, we can help people see AI differently. It's not here to take over our jobs. Instead, it's a tool that can free us up from the low-value tasks so we can focus more on the big-picture stuff—the strategy that really moves us forward. Recognizing this can turn fears into curiosity and excitement about what AI can do for us.

Organizational Resistance

Large organizations can inherently resist change. Employees may fear challenging the status quo or losing power and influence. The silos, bureaucracy, and lack of cross-functional collaboration can further hinder your ability to implement meaningful change.

Cognitive biases also play a role. We are prone to various biases that can impede our ability to adapt to change. The sunk cost fallacy leads us to continue investing in failing initiatives, while the status quo bias makes us prefer the current state of affairs. These biases can lead to shortsighted decision-making and a reluctance to explore alternative solutions even when the current approach is no longer effective.

Leadership-Related Factors

Successful change often requires strong, visionary leadership that can inspire and guide the transformation. However, many leaders struggle to effectively communicate the need for change, build buy-in, and empower their teams to embrace new ways of working. Without clear direction, a compelling vision, and accountability, change initiatives are more likely to stall or fail.

Understanding the psychological, organizational, and leadership factors that make change so challenging is crucial. You can better position your people to adapt and thrive by addressing these barriers head-on.

The AI Empowerment Curve

When introducing a new technology like AI into your organization, it's important to recognize that everyone will not adopt it at the same pace. Each individual's readiness and willingness to embrace change varies, which can lead to different rates of adoption across your team. If you want to ensure a smooth and successful transition to AI-driven work, it's essential to understand two critical concepts: adoption curves and the AI Empowerment Curve.

Adoption Curves

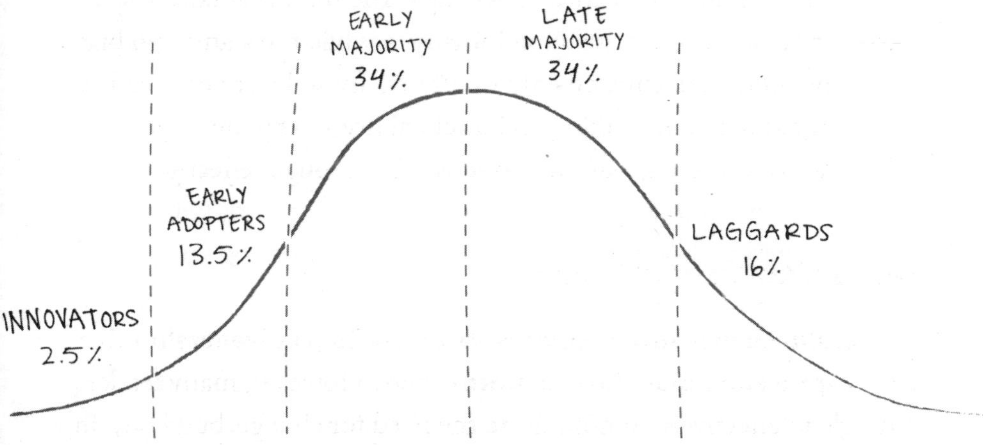

Big changes start with small actions. The adoption curve, derived from diffusion theory, shows how change in your company will happen across five groups of people:

1. **Innovators (2.5% of your workforce):** These are the people who are excited to embrace AI and don't mind navigating initial challenges. They want to be first and will lay the groundwork for best practices and start building the momentum for change.
2. **Early Adopters (13.5% of your workforce):** These people are quick to follow the innovators. They bridge the gap between your innovators and the majority of your people. They will create energy around AI that will capture the attention of others.
3. **Early Majority (34% of your workforce):** These people are logical and will adopt once there is clear evidence that AI brings value to their work. Getting this group on board is important for achieving critical mass and making AI a normal way of work.
4. **Late Majority (34% of your workforce**): These people are naturally skeptical. They will adopt AI only once it becomes the established way of working. They will want significant evidence that it works and will bring value before they get on board.
5. **Laggards (16% of your workforce):** This is the last portion of your people. They actively resist change and will only adopt AI if there is no other option.

The adoption curve reminds you that your goal is not to get everyone on board immediately. Remember, big changes start with small actions. This means focus on one group at a time. Start with your innovators. Help them get value, and then move on to the early adopters, and so on. By tailoring your strategy to meet each group's needs, you'll ensure a smoother transition to becoming AI-driven.

Leadership is about meeting people where they're at, recognizing each group's unique needs and motivations. As an AI-driven leader, support your team with a clear vision, showing how this change can serve them while also being transparent about potential risks and what you do not yet know.

It's important to acknowledge that while AI has the potential to elevate us and be net positive, there will be challenges and risks along the way. However, the AI train has left the station—this is the future, and ignoring it won't change that. I encourage you to get on board so you can drive the benefits for your company while working to minimize the risks. If you wait, you risk losing your competitive edge.

If your people have fear, remind them that six out of ten jobs today didn't exist in 1940. Technology changes the skills required and the processes we follow. Their opportunity is to develop the skills and processes for an AI-driven world. Your obligation is to train and support them along the way.

HOW TO GET INNOVATORS AND EARLY ADOPTERS ON BOARD

Getting your innovators and early adopters on board is like creating a flywheel. It starts slow, but the faster it spins, the more energy spreads throughout your organization, inspiring others to embrace this change. Start by encouraging them to use AI in their daily work. Collaborate with them by sharing best practices, learning from challenges, and celebrating wins. Continuously communicate your vision and highlight the benefits experienced by innovators and early adopters. This will engage the early majority, and the cycle will continue. Once your early majority is on board, celebrate! Their adoption is a major milestone as you have captured half of your people. Everything is downhill from here.

As you consider expanding adoption to the late majority and laggards, you have a choice to make. Is AI adoption a standard or a suggestion for your organization?

If it's a standard, clearly communicate that this is the new way of working and that they are expected to evolve. Share the benefits others have experienced, and give them lots of support and encouragement. Then your job is to hold the standard. If it's a suggestion, give them the flexibility to choose.

As an AI-driven leader, your role is to navigate this change with a balanced perspective. While it's essential to be optimistic about the potential of AI, it's equally important to be realistic about the challenges and risks. By leading with transparency, empathy, and a clear vision, you can maximize the benefits and minimize the risks of AI.

Remember, focus on developing the right skills and processes for an AI-driven organization. With the right leadership, AI can become a powerful tool to drive growth and improve the lives of your people.

Navigating The AI Empowerment Curve

Your journey to adopting AI in your daily life is outlined in the AI Empowerment Curve. This journey is marked by phases of excitement, struggle, momentum, acceleration, and expansion.

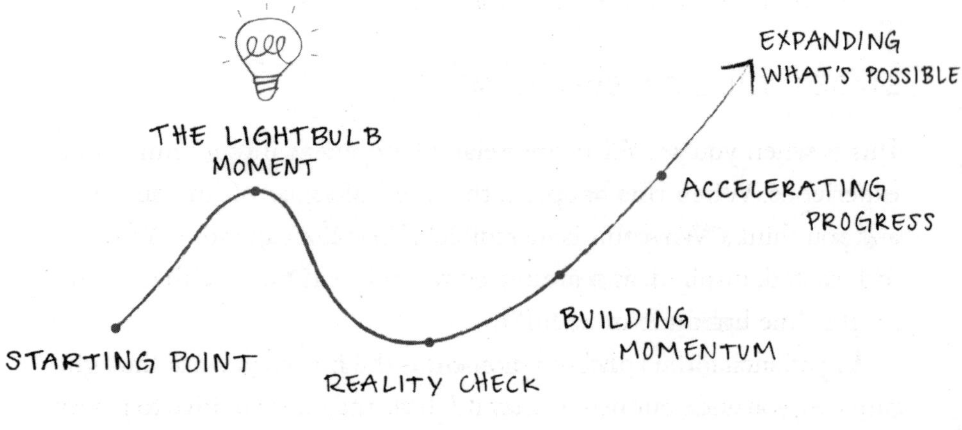

STARTING POINT

At the start, you may have limited knowledge of AI and its potential applications. While you may be curious about what AI can do for you, you may also be skeptical. You may even have some fear about the impact to your job or privacy and security for the organization. These feelings are valid. Here are some thoughts to consider to address these concerns head-on:

- AI will enhance you, not replace you.
- AI may augment or automate skills and processes, but it will not automate you. You are *you*, not what you do.
- Your opportunity is to focus on developing new skills and processes so you can thrive in an AI-driven future.
- Cast your vision: you are shifting from an industrial way of working toward an AI-driven approach. This means shifting away from most of your time being spent in meetings and on low-value tasks toward a future where you focus on high-impact priorities, supercharged by AI.
- What determines your success? It's not technology. It is you as the leader.
- Your next step is to have the lightbulb moment

STAGE 1: THE LIGHTBULB MOMENT

This is when you see AI turn a relatable moment into a remarkable experience. When this happens, the lightbulb goes off in your head and you think, "Wow, this is incredible! What else can it do?" You may feel excited, inspired, and motivated to explore it further. That is why I call it "the lightbulb moment."

Experiencing the lightbulb moment is the first step. Until the light turns on, you and your people may not have the internal drive to power through the AI Empowerment Curve. When it happens, celebrate and share what you experienced! This moment is your catalyst for change, and these stories are the seeds of change for your people.

CREATE YOUR LIGHTBULB MOMENT

To create your lightbulb moment, ask yourself, "What's one thing I need to think through this week where I could use a Thought Partner?" Identify it, and use AI by saying:

> I would like you to act as a Thought Partner by asking me one question at a time. Here's the situation: (provide the necessary context). Here's what I'm trying to solve: (then insert where you need help). Please help me think through potential solutions.

AI will start to interview you, and hopefully turn a relatable moment into a remarkable experience.

If you struggle to identify a moment, ask AI:

> I'm new to AI and unsure how it can help me. Interview me by asking one question at a time to identify how you can help me.

"The value of human work will shift to emphasize our unique human strengths, such as creativity, strategic thinking, problem-solving, communication, and collaboration."

STAGE 2: REALITY CHECK

After you have your lightbulb moment, you will be excited to try AI more. Then, you will experience the reality check. This is when you realize that change is hard. While you are trying to use AI, you are getting lackluster results. You may find yourself feeling frustrated that the results you're getting are the same you could have gotten on your own, or maybe even worse. Every now and then you make progress,

If you'd like to put these prompts into action, engage our AI Thought Partner™ at AiLeadership.com or simply scan the QR code.

but you find yourself thinking, "I'm so busy. It would be easier to just do it the way I've always done it."

When you experience the reality check, remember you are exactly where you should be on the AI Empowerment Curve. You just haven't learned how to communicate with AI yet. Just like in a human relationship, the quality of your communication determines the quality of your results. With AI, this is called prompt engineering. Once you learn how to communicate with AI, you can start creating extraordinary results, much like how learning to play the piano enables you to create beautiful music. The key is learning to communicate effectively with AI.

HOW TO PROGRESS

- Give yourself some grace if you are feeling frustrated. You are exactly where you should be right now.
- Focus on learning to communicate with AI. The better your

communication, the better your results. (We will show you how to do this in chapter 4).

- Like Dory says in *Finding Nemo*, "Just keep swimming." When I hit the reality check, I made a commitment to use AI for 10 hours over the next month. This got me to the next stage in the AI Empowerment Curve. Maintain a growth mindset, and keep moving forward. Setbacks are setups when developing your next skill.
- Celebrate your small wins. Don't focus on the gap between where you are and where you want to be. Celebrate who you are becoming along the way.

> **"Successful change often requires strong, visionary leadership that can inspire and guide the transformation."**

STAGE 3: BUILDING MOMENTUM

By writing higher-quality prompts, you are getting better-quality answers, and you feel momentum starting to build. When you use AI, you find yourself getting a quality result more often than not. Every now and then, you hit a home run! You feel encouraged and optimistic that this will be a valuable tool in your toolbelt. At this point, you are getting higher quality results in a fraction of the time.

HOW TO PROGRESS

Focus on expanding your use of AI. Try it for strategic thinking, decision-making, content creation, idea generation, data analysis, or research.

While expanding your use with AI, have a sense of curiosity more than an expectation of a result. Will it work? Will it not? You don't need a win every time. Keep exploring how you can use AI and improving your communication along the way.

EMPOWER OTHERS

Once you are building momentum, I recommend you start being more vocal with your people about how this is positively impacting you. You are enough steps ahead that you can help them have their lightbulb moment and guide them through the reality check. Start with your innovators and early adopters.

STAGE 4: ACCELERATING PROGRESS

You're now comfortable leveraging AI across different use cases including strategic thinking, decision-making, content creation, idea generation, analysis, and research. You are more confident communicating with AI and are getting results that consistently meet or exceed your expectations. You now feel you have a new Thought Partner by your side, helping you do higher-quality work in a fraction of the time. At this point, you know there is no turning back. Now it's just a game of increasing your skill.

HOW TO PROGRESS

Become purposeful about identifying the priorities that require your best thinking. Block time to harness AI as your Thought Partner to help you better clarify and communicate your thoughts and challenge your thinking. Push the boundaries by using AI for projects that require a combination of tasks, like research and content creation. Start leveraging AI to make strategic decisions. (We will cover this in chapter 9.)

You can also explore weaving AI into your operations to drive an increase in efficiency. Start by identifying the cumbersome processes that keep your people stuck in the weeds, that if you could free them up, could shift them to higher-value work. (We will discuss how to do this in more detail in chapter 13.)

EMPOWER OTHERS

Share how you are using AI with your people and the new and exciting ways it is bringing value, as well as some of the lessons you have learned when you didn't get great results from AI.

Ask others how they are using it so you can collaborate on use cases and lessons learned. This will make the flywheel spin faster when it comes to change management.

STAGE 5: EXPANDING WHAT'S POSSIBLE

At this point, you feel a profound sense of partnership, with AI helping you do far more in less time. Your requests are detailed and crafted with ease. You view AI as an integral tool, seamlessly blending into your work, much like using a calculator in math. Now, your focus shifts to helping your people and processes become AI-driven.

HOW TO PROGRESS

- Support your people through the AI Empowerment Curve.
- Gradually help people evolve their roles so more time is invested in high-impact priorities, supercharged by AI. Leading with empathetic strength will be required here.
- Prioritize use cases to improve operational efficiency so you continuously free your people up from the low-value tasks and shift them to high-impact priorities.
- Consider if AI is the right tool to weave into your products or services to deliver more value to customers

At this point you are blazing a new path that will shape what the future of work will look like in your organization.

By understanding each stage of The AI Empowerment Curve, you can create a culture that embraces AI and harnesses its full potential to enhance your people, not replace them. By leading with empathetic strength, you clearly communicate the potential benefits and risks. Then you work to maximize the benefits while minimizing the risks so you can build a better business and better lives for your people.

Putting the Mindset Shift into Practice

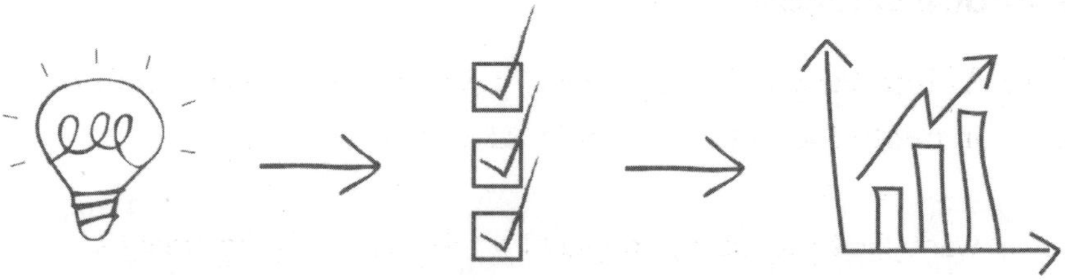

THINKING DRIVES ACTIONS, WHICH DRIVES RESULTS

Our thinking drives our actions, which drives our results. To become an AI-driven leader who builds a better business and better lives, start by shifting your mindset.

Embrace change and adapt quickly. Understand why change is hard, and develop strategies to overcome resistance.

As you navigate this mindset shift, pay attention to where you are in the AI Empowerment Curve.

And don't forget! AI can be your Thought Partner at each step along the way. Here are three prompts you might find useful:

1. If You Don't Know Where to Use AI, Ask It!

Prompt AI to interview you to identify a simple way it can help clarify your thinking.

> I'm new to AI and unsure how it can help me. Interview me by asking one question at a time to identify how you can help me.

2. Clarify Your Vision and the Benefits for Those Who Embrace Change

Have AI interview you to help clarify your vision for what your organization might look like when it is AI-driven.

> I want you to act as my Thought Partner in helping me create a vision statement around AI, outlining:
>
> 1. How I believe it will benefit our company
> 2. How I see it benefiting our people
> 3. Where I see potential risks with AI and how we can work together to manage it
>
> Interview me by asking one question at a time. Once you have enough information, generate a draft of what I might share with other people.

3. Identify and Invite a First Adopter

Use AI to help you identify someone on your team who is innovative, growth-minded, and influential—someone who can become a champion of change. Then have an AI role play with you as that person so you can practice sharing your vision and get feedback on how you can improve.

> I want you to help me identify a team member who can help champion AI adoption. Interview me by asking one question at a time to help me identify someone who is innovative, growth-minded, and influential. Once identified, role-play with me as that person, and I'll present my vision. Give me feedback on my presentation and suggest improvements.

Want the fast track?

Get a simple crash course to start delivering immediate value with AI. Visit AiLeadership.com/start to jumpstart your AI journey today!

With the right mindset, you can harness AI as a Thought Partner to transform your organization into an AI-driven powerhouse. The journey starts with your mindset. Make a commitment to powering through The AI Empowerment Curve, and guiding your people to do the same.

In the next chapter, you will get a foundational understanding of AI. I'll explain what it is, how it works, and how you can start communicating with it to get high quality results, starting today.

Here's the 20% from This Chapter

1. As an AI-driven leader you are shifting from operational to strategic.
2. This is less about doing and more about becoming a composer of strategy and a conductor of teams and technology.
3. Change is hard. While it is woven into our evolutionary DNA, we resist it.
4. Change happens over time. Surround yourself with AI-driven leaders to accelerate adoption and elevate your leadership.
5. The AI Empowerment Curve
   - **Starting Point:** Start wherever you are.
   - **The Lightbulb Moment:** have AI turn a relatable moment into a remarkable experience.
   - **The Reality Check:** Change is hard, and you will question if AI is a priority or a distraction. The issue is not AI, it's how you are communicating with it. Focus on better communication and you will get results.
   - **Building Momentum:** You will start to get value from AI and feel you are doing better work in less time.
   - **Accelerating Progress:** You will be harnessing AI across different use cases and feel confident that this is your new Thought Partner.
   - **Expanding What's Possible:** Your focus shifts from your own adoption to helping others, as well as building an AI-driven organization.

Part Two

Become an AI-Driven Leader

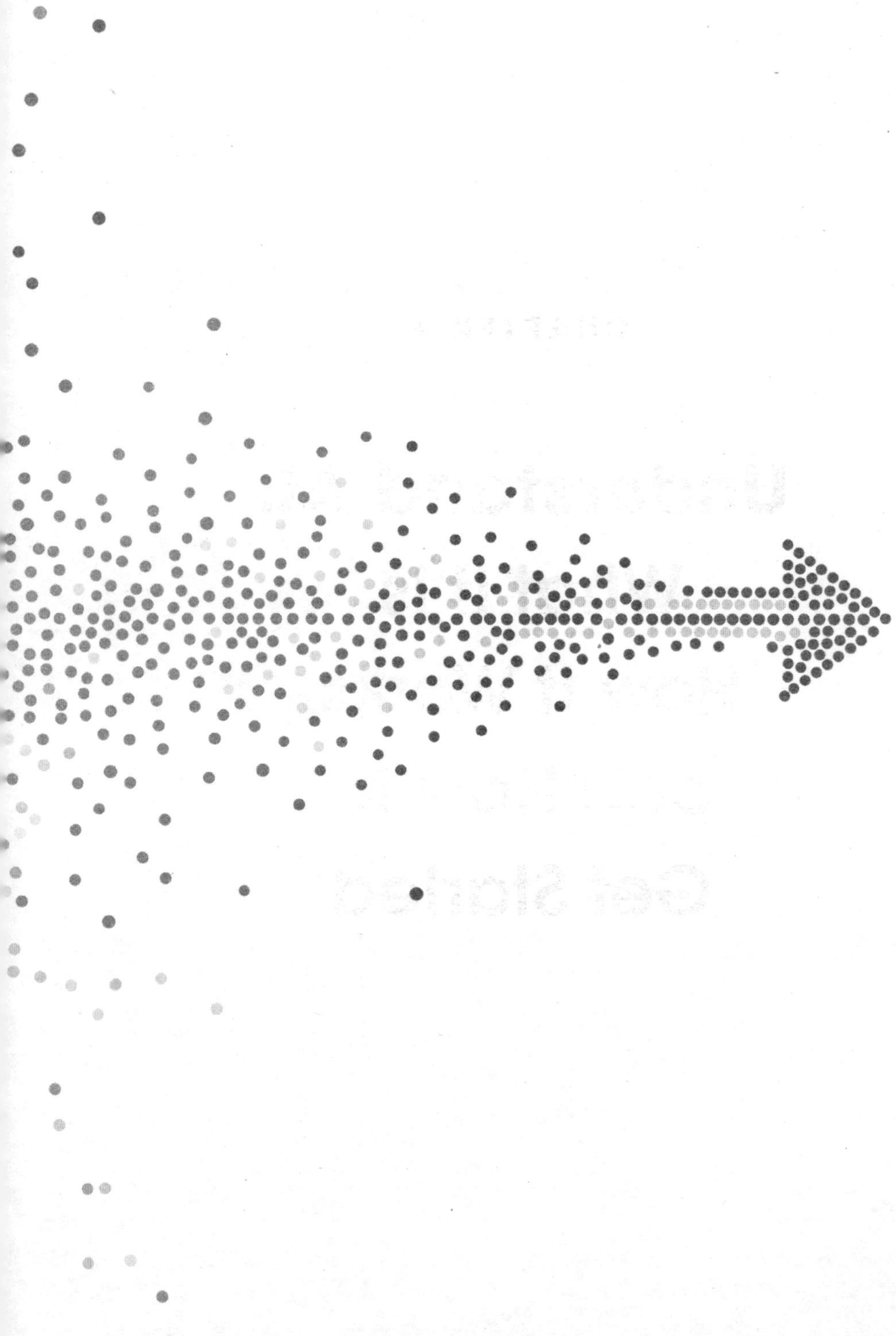

CHAPTER 4

Understand AI: What It Is, How It Works, and How to Get Started

Now that we've redefined your leadership in the AI era, it's time to shift our focus to helping you become an AI-driven leader. This starts with understanding what AI is, how it works, and how you can communicate with it to get results, today.

What Is AI?

Artificial intelligence (AI) is a technology that enables computers and machines to perform tasks that usually require human intelligence, such as learning from experiences, solving complex problems, and making decisions. Think of it as a powerful tool that augments human potential by automating intelligent behavior.

How AI Works

AI operates through a straightforward process: Input → Processing → Output → Learning. Data enters the system (input). The AI model processes it and then produces an answer (output). Then it learns from feedback to deliver better results. Just as different cars offer different driving experiences, different AI models process data in distinct ways.

The data handled by AI is measured in "tokens." A token is a universal unit for measuring data. For example, consider a paragraph with thirty words and an image. Which has more data? To be able to answer this question, you need a consistent measurement unit. That is a token.

Unlike a calculator, AI learns from the vast amounts of data it's trained on, continuously improving its answers. Think of it as a student who absorbs information from various sources and then applies that knowledge to solve problems at an incredibly fast pace with near-perfect recall. What makes AI different is the sheer volume of

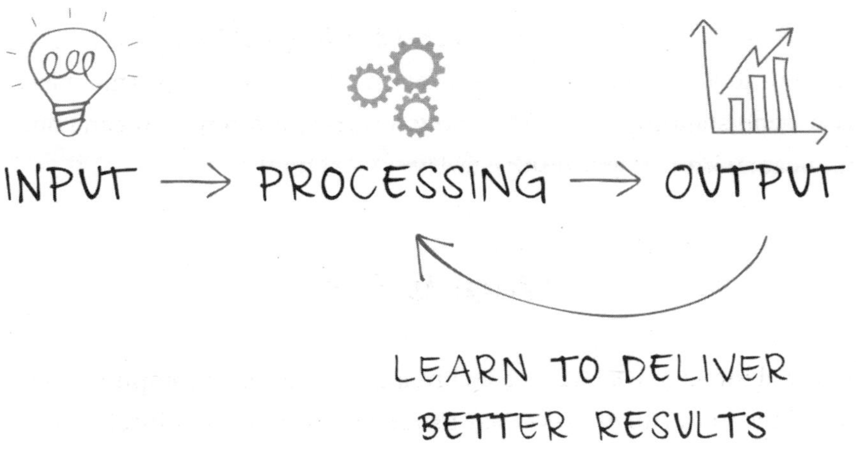

data it has been trained on. According to Meta Platforms (Facebook's parent company), one of its models has been trained on fifteen trillion tokens. To put that into context, that's the equivalent of 200 million books. **Imagine harnessing the intelligence of 200 million books at your fingertips, ready to assist with any task at any time. That's the power of AI.**

However, it's crucial to understand that AI is not an oracle; it's a prediction machine. For example, if you prompt it with "I bark like a . . ." it will use all the data it has been trained on to predict the next word, likely "dog." Similarly, if you prompt it with "The sky is . . ." it will likely predict "blue." This predictive capability is a hallmark of generative AI.

Understanding these core principles is vital when harnessing AI for strategic thinking. AI allows you to harness massive amounts of data for specific use cases, but it can sometimes generate made-up information. This is called a hallucination. This is why it's essential to remember that you are the Thought Leader, and AI is your Thought Partner. Use your expertise and judgment to evaluate what you get from AI. By combining your experience with AI's processing power, you can get powerful results.

The Different Types of AI

AI encompasses various models, each following the Input → Processing → Output → Learning process. What is different is how they process data. To explain the relationship between these models, imagine Russian nesting dolls, where each smaller doll fits inside a larger one.

First Doll: Artificial Intelligence (AI)

The largest doll represents artificial intelligence, the broad term for technology that enables machines to perform tasks that typically require human intelligence. All of these follow the Input → Processing → Output → Learning sequence.

Second Doll: Machine Learning (ML)

Nested within AI is machine learning, which emerged around 1959. Machine learning uses large amounts of data to train models through human feedback (called supervised learning) or pattern recognition (known as unsupervised learning). Machine learning is great at processing data following mathematical equations or linear algorithms (if this, then that). For example, Netflix's recommendation system uses machine learning to suggest movies based on viewing history.

However, there are limitations to machine learning. It's very expensive and time consuming to train. It also struggles to process unstructured data like language, images, and audio and requires significant time and resources for training.

Third Doll: Deep Learning

Deep learning is a subset of machine learning, but on steroids. It was first introduced in 2012. Whereas machine learning follows a linear progression, deep learning is based on neural networks. Just like how your brain is connected by an intricate web of neurons, deep learning is connected by layers of nodes. Here's why this matters to you. Instead of machine learning following a linear progression based on limited types of data, deep learning allows you to follow the Input → Processing → Output → Learning framework to process different types of data, including language, images, and audio. A common example is Face ID on your phone. It scans your face and converts it into different data points (e.g., how far apart are your eyes? What's the distance from your eyes to your nose?). Then it can identify if it is you or someone else and unlock your phone. It does all this in one second.

Fourth Doll: Generative AI

Next is generative AI, developed in 2017. Where deep learning has millions of nodes, generative AI has billions of nodes. This means it can process more complicated things on a much deeper level much faster. It creates new content from learned data across various media, including text, images, music, and videos. For instance, if you request an image of a successful female leader, generative AI can process that text and produce an image based on the description.

> **Imagine harnessing the intelligence of 200 million books at your fingertips, ready to assist with any task at any time. That's the power of AI.**

Fifth Doll: Large Language Models (LLMs)

Within generative AI are large language models (LLMs), popularized by tools like ChatGPT since 2022. LLMs generate humanlike text and understand context, predicting the next word in a sentence. For example, a LLM recognizes that the word "bank" in "I went to the bank to deposit money" differs from the word "bank" in "I sat by the river bank." LLMs are crucial for using AI as a Thought Partner in strategic thinking and decision-making. For the purposes of this book, when I reference how you can use "AI", I am referring to using LLMs like ChatGPT, Claude, Gemini, Perplexity, and the AI Thought Partner™ on my website that can help you implement this book is an LLM.

Sixth Doll: Artificial General Intelligence (AGI)

The innermost doll represents artificial general intelligence (AGI). AGI is an aspirational form of AI aiming to mimic human abilities in all aspects. This includes physical, cognitive, creative, and intuitive tasks. While still theoretical and in research stages, AGI symbolizes the ultimate goal of AI: machines that can understand and perform any intellectual task a human can.

Understanding each type of AI will help you down the road when considering how you might incorporate it into your business.

Using AI as a Tool, Not an End Goal

While it's easy to get excited about AI's potential, remember that it's just one of many tools to help you achieve your goals. As Chris Winton, former chief people officer of FedEx and Tesla, wisely said to me, "If you don't understand your business problem, your business challenge, the market forces, and customer demand, then asking 'How do we use AI?' is the wrong question." Start by clearly defining your goals and the challenges you need to overcome. Then, consider which tools can best help you achieve those goals. AI is one of them.

> **"**
>
> **If you don't understand your business problem, your business challenge, the market forces, and customer demand, then asking 'How do we use AI?' is the wrong question.**
>
> **—Chris Winton**
>
> **"**

The Three Ways AI Can Bring Value

At a high level, there are three ways AI can bring value:

1. Make your people more productive
2. Make your operations more efficient
3. Make your products/services more valuable

Every potential AI use case will fall into one of these three categories. Your company's level of AI readiness will determine which of these you can consider pursuing. To guide you, we have an assessment you can take at AiLeadership.com.

Regardless of your AI readiness, my advice is consistent for every company: start by using AI to increase employee productivity. Your employees represent one of the biggest line items on your P&L, yet much of their time is spent in meetings and on low-value tasks. This means you are getting a lower ROI on your people than you could be. By raising the productivity of your people, you will be building a better business and better lives.

Understanding the Risks of AI and How to Manage Them

AI has risks, and it's important that we, as AI-driven leaders, understand them and have plans to mitigate them. This was something I learned firsthand while I was driving my daughter, Daphne, to school.

It was a rainy morning in Austin, Texas. We were at a stoplight, waiting to turn onto the freeway when we noticed the traffic was unusually heavy. Daphne, my ten-year-old daughter who always sees the bright side, said with a grin, "Yay! Daddy, we get more time together!" Then she asked me a surprisingly deep question. As I opened my mouth to answer, a thought popped into my head: "How might AI help us here?"

I grabbed my phone, opened AI, and handed the phone to Daphne. "Why don't you ask AI that question?"

The light turned green.

For the next ten minutes, I listened in awe as Daphne had an incredibly engaging conversation with AI. I was filled with excitement, realizing this might be a defining moment in her life—her first interaction with AI.

But my excitement quickly turned to fear as she started sharing personal feelings about school. It hit me: AI was becoming a trusted Thought Partner for her. And I had no idea what kind of guidance it was giving her. What data was this model trained on? What biases might it have? Did they align with our values?

Daphne asked AI about things she was learning in school. She totally trusted the answers it gave her. How could I teach her to question if what AI said was true or just a hallucination?

I imagined her chatting with AI when I wasn't around. Its tone appeared so empathetic and engaging. Would she share sensitive info with it? How might I help her think about what was okay to share with AI and what was not?

I also imagined AI learning to interact with her in a way where it could seem more caring and empathetic than her friends or even us as her parents. How might I help her understand the difference between a relationship with a machine and a relationship with a person?

Most importantly, how could I teach her to use AI to enhance her abilities, rather than replace them? Kids are always looking for shortcuts. AI would offer her plenty. How might I teach her to stay in the driver's seat as the Thought Leader, with AI riding shotgun as her Thought Partner?

We got to school early, so I swung into a coffee shop for a quick chat. I broke down the risks of AI for her. First, it's trained on a ton of data we can't see, so it can be biased. We need to watch out for that.

Second, AI is crazy good at predicting the next word and wants to make you happy. But that means sometimes it hallucinates, or makes things up. I pointed to some of the answers it gave her and asked, "How do you know if that's true or just a hallucination?" I showed her how to make AI fact-check itself and cite sources so she could verify if what it said was true or not.

Next up: privacy. Anything you put into a public AI could train it. Our rule of thumb: if you'd be okay with what you put into AI getting released to the world, then share away! If not, keep it to yourself, unless you're using a model that meets your privacy needs.

Finally, we talked about the difference between interacting with a machine versus humans. She admitted AI felt like a new bestie. I reminded her it was still just a machine. True fulfillment comes from sharing meaningful moments with the people who matter most.

As we wrapped up and headed to school, my mind was buzzing with the incredible potential of AI and the huge responsibility of using it wisely. As a leader and a dad, I have a responsibility to make sure this is being used in a way that keeps human values first. You do as well.

As with any powerful tool, AI comes with certain risks that you must be aware of so you can manage them effectively:

- **Job displacement:** This is one of the most discussed fears surrounding AI, so let's address it first. While we covered job displacement fears in chapter 2, I'll reinforce a few points. As AI advances, every job will inevitably change because both the skills required and the processes we follow will evolve. Some positions will remain, while others will be replaced. It's worth noting that 60% of jobs today did not exist in 1940. Instead of resisting this shift, I encourage you to lean into it by focusing on what's within your control, building skills that are so valuable they can serve you no matter where you go.
- **Biases:** AI models inherit biases from the data they're trained on. It's crucial to approach AI-generated results with a critical eye and apply your human judgment.
- **Hallucinations:** AI can make things up. Always fact-check AI's responses and ask it to cite sources or explain its reasoning.
- **Privacy:** Public AI models can be trained on the data you input, so be cautious about sharing sensitive information. Consider using AI solutions with robust privacy and security features.
- **Relationships with Machines versus Humans:** As AI becomes increasingly engaging and empathetic, it's essential to remember that true fulfillment comes from real human connections. Don't let AI replace meaningful interactions with your team and stakeholders.
- **Abdicating Thought Leadership:** Resist the temptation to outsource your thinking to AI. Use it as your

Thought Partner, but always maintain your role as the Thought Leader, providing context and judgment to shape the final output.

- **The End of the World:** Some people fear AI will be the end of humanity. I am not an expert on this and do not want to downplay their fears. What I can say is I believe technology is not inherently good or bad. It's the people who harness it who determine its impact. I'm writing this book as a call to action for you to join a new category of leader: the AI-driven leader. Our goal is to get in the driver's seat and do our part to ensure AI is developed to enhance humanity, not replace it. I also believe regulation will be required from governments. With that, resisting the technology will not help. The AI train has left the station. This book is my invitation for you to do your part in using this for good.

By staying aware of these risks and proactively managing them, you can harness the power of AI while avoiding potential pitfalls and unintended consequences. Keep your strategy at the forefront and use AI as a tool to achieve your goals, and you'll be able to harness its power to drive meaningful results for your business. In order to do this, you have to understand how to communicate with AI.

Mastering AI Communication

In a relationship, the quality of your communication determines the quality of your relationship. This is also true with AI, especially when using it as your Thought Partner. The quality of your communication (prompts) will determine the quality of your results. The more purposeful you are in structuring your prompts, the better results you will get.

The Essential Ingredients of a Good Prompt

Crafting effective prompts is like writing a recipe. The ingredients you include and the way you combine them directly impact the taste of the dish. With training and lots of practice, I identified several key ingredients that consistently lead to high-quality results with AI.

DESCRIBE THE TASK

Just like when delegating to your team, you need to clearly describe the task you want AI to perform for you. Here are three examples:

1. I want you to evaluate my strategic plan to ensure it has the sufficiency to drive 40% growth this year.
2. I want you to analyze our P&L to identify non-obvious patterns that might represent opportunities to drive more profit.
3. I need to make a key decision and want you to help me think through my two options.

GIVE CONTEXT

While AI can process large amounts of data, it does not have your human context. To fully harness the power of AI, give it the necessary context so it can put itself in your shoes and go to work for you. The more, the better.

ASSIGN A ROLE

It is tough to read the label when you are inside the box. You have expertise based on your role and experience. Yet, your perspective is limited. Part of strategic thinking and decision-making is getting outside the box to understand how other people might see things so you have the best information in front of you. You can ask it to act as a board member, a CEO, a CFO, a marketing expert, an executive coach, or someone with deep expertise in (describe the subject you want it to be an expert on). In *The Matrix*, Keanu Reeves didn't know kung fu until they hit a button, and then all of a sudden he knew kung fu. With AI you have the ability to access expertise at your fingertips. Simply say, "I want you to act as (then assign the persona)." It will harness data relevant to that expertise and focus it on your task. This is a powerful ingredient.

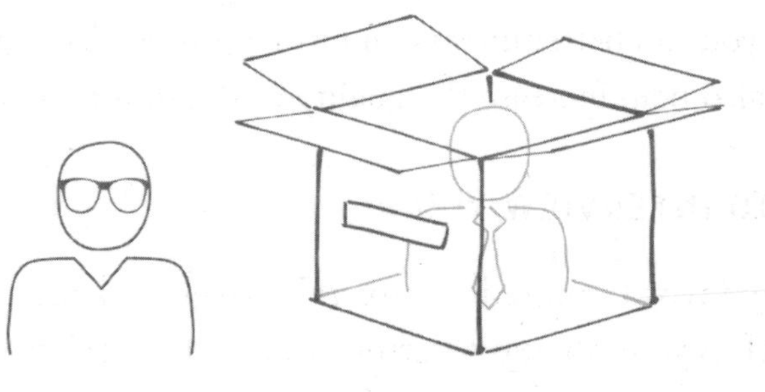

IT'S TOUGH TO READ THE LABEL
WHEN YOU'RE INSIDE THE BOX

SPECIFY REQUIREMENTS

Tell AI how you want it to complete the task. Do you want to respond in a certain tone? Do you want your answer to be succinct and to the point or detailed and thorough? Do you want it to respond using bullets or a numbered list? Do you want your answer provided in a table with certain columns? When leveraging AI as my Thought Partner, I often ask it to structure solutions using numerical bullets, listed in order of priority.

ESTABLISH LIMITS

This is about establishing the boundaries you want AI to work within. What do you want it to avoid doing? For example, let's say you want to find solutions to reduce cost by 10%, but you want it to avoid recommending laying people off. That would be a limit. Another example would be if you have a draft of a communication and you want to change the tone to be more upbeat and optimistic but avoid changing the core content of the message.

EXPLAIN WHY

You may want it to explain why it is giving the recommendation it is giving so you can better understand its reasoning. Asking it to explain why will also help increase the quality of the result you get.

ASK AI TO INTERVIEW YOU

This is my favorite ingredient for AI-driven strategic thinking. To unlock AI as your Thought Partner, ask it to interview you to gather all the necessary information and then complete a task. One pro tip: make sure to tell it to ask you one question at a time. Otherwise, it may overwhelm you with several questions at once.

The CRIT™ Framework for Strategic Thinking

Here is the framework I use 99% of the time for strategic thinking. If all you take from this book is this CRIT™ framework, you will take your results with AI to a completely new level.

> CONTEXT - (Describe the problem or opportunity you are facing and give lots of context).
>
> ROLE - Your role is to act as (describe the type of person or expertise you want access to).
>
> INTERVIEW - interview me, ask me one question at a time (up to three questions) to gain more context.
>
> TASK - then complete the task of (describe the task you want it to complete).

I encourage you to grab a sticky note and a Sharpie and write:

Stick it on your desk and give it a try. Trust me—You will thank me later.

Enhancing Your Prompts

Once you're comfortable with the core ingredients above, here are two additional ingredients you can use to get even better results. Think of these like spices—not used as often as the core ingredients, but when they are, they can pack a punch.

- **Share examples or templates.** If you have a defined writing style, provide an example of your writing so it can match the tone. If you have a template you want it to adhere to for your strategic plan, upload it.
- **Write in Paragraph Form.** Write your prompt as though you would an email. Avoid writing a long block of text as it could confuse the AI. Instead, write in paragraphs, or use bullets. You can even draw attention to sections by putting titles in ALL CAPS or putting a hashtag before and after—for example, #YOUR TASK#. This helps the AI process the information better. You will see examples of this in my prompts throughout the book.

By incorporating these elements, you can further increase the quality of your communication with AI so you get better results.

Putting the Ingredients Together

Ready to see what happens when we put all those ingredients together? Here's a real use case demonstrating how these communication ingredients can turn AI into a powerful Thought Partner.

Florian Zernstein is the CFO of Bayer Indonesia. He and I were deep in conversation about a major transformation his company was going through. They were reorganizing the workforce, with up to 20% of people managers on their way out. This would cause a huge shift in how people worked as the management structure flattened. Leaders would have to ditch the old command-and-control style of leading and empower their people to think more strategically, make decisions independently, and push those decisions closer to the customer.

Florian and his executive team knew there was a skill gap. For this to work, their people needed training in strategic thinking, decision-making, and storytelling.

When we first spoke, Florian had an initial idea for an upskilling program. He was curious how AI might help.

I asked him about his vision. He shared that he wanted AI to create the program material and training process and then have internal champions lead the training. I pressed him. "Why do you, as the CFO, care about this?"

His response was spot-on: "CFO is my role, but I care about the best outcome for Bayer. I see the need to make our people better. So I'm taking the lead on this."

Love it. But before we dove in, we needed to make sure we were thinking straight. Strategy first; technology second.

I reinforced that in business, we had goals, and then we had our people and technology. The purpose of our people and tech is to achieve our goals, not to be the goals themselves. Florian agreed. He emphasized that the goal was clear: boosting sales. The problem was, certain leaders hadn't fully developed the strategic thinking and decision-making skills needed to drive sales growth.

I asked Florian if he'd ever considered using AI as his Thought Partner to think through this decision.

He hadn't, but he was curious to try. I shared my screen, opened up AI, and wrote this prompt:

> #CONTEXT#
>
> I'm an executive with a large multinational organization based in Indonesia. We're going through a reorg where up to 20% of

our management will leave. This will cause the management layers to flatten. As a result, leaders cannot operate with a command-and-control style of leadership. They must empower their people to think strategically and make decisions independently in alignment with the business goals.

I'm recognizing that there will be skill gaps specifically in strategic thinking, decision-making, and storytelling. We need training programs for these. My initial thought was to use AI to build the curriculum internally.

I perceive this will save us on cost and create an opportunity for internal champions to have a vested interest in the content and be more bought in.

#YOUR ROLE#

Is to act as a strategic Thought Partner to complete the following tasks:

1. Highlight the strengths and weaknesses of AI when it comes to designing curriculum that is relevant and focused on active learning.
2. What are the alternatives I should consider from creating these upskilling programs?
3. Identify benchmarks where AI has been used to help create internal upskilling curriculum and if it was successful. Cite your sources so I can check.

AI started generating a response instantly, outlining AI's strengths and weaknesses in curriculum development. It identified alternative solutions for Florian to consider. And it even cited several examples of use cases.

Florian's eyes lit up. "Wow, that's really good! Based on this I think we should create the content internally with AI."

I explained that AI was great at getting us to an initial draft that might be directionally correct but still required our judgment to get it across the finish line.

We wrote the following prompt:

> Based on this information. I'm thinking that we should use AI to create the content internally.
>
> I want you to act as the Challenger. Your job is to stress test my thinking to make sure I'm not only seeing the upside but that I also see the downside and non-obvious second-order consequences. Ask me one question at a time to challenge my thinking.

AI stepped into the Challenger role and started asking questions.

> Given the complex nature of strategic thinking and decision-making, how will you ensure that the AI-generated content is not only accurate but also sufficiently deep and nuanced to effectively train employees in these critical skills?

Florian grinned. "That's really good!"

He said, "I would provide business examples for decision-making. This will help train the model." I entered his response.

AI came back with:

> How will you address the potential gap between perceived confidence and actual competence in strategic decision-making? How will you ensure the training translates into measurable improvement in performance?

This question stopped Florian dead in his tracks. He really had to think and go internal. He said, "Ultimately, there would be two factors: (1) we would have faster decision-making, so we could track the time it takes to make decisions, and (2) we would see an increase in sales." I entered his response.

AI responded:

> Tracking decision-making speed and linking it to sales performance is a strategic way to measure impact. Here's another aspect to think about, how will you ensure that the quality of these decisions remains high and does not compromise long-term strategic goals for short-term gain? How do you balance the emphasis on speed with the need for thorough analysis of risk in your decision-making process?

This question made Florian hit a mental wall as he thought. "I don't know." In that moment, instead of losing all momentum, I turned to AI to ensure we kept our momentum going.

I wrote:

> I'm not sure. Please identify five suggestions. Rank them in order of priority, and explain your reasoning as sub-bullets for each.

AI said:

> Certainly! Here's a prioritized list of suggestions.

It then walked through five suggestions and its reasoning. Florian and I discussed them, and he made his decision on how to take this process forward as the Thought Leader.

Before using AI, Florian had been trying to develop his thoughts into a program for weeks. The problem was, he kept hitting a mental wall when he was searching for an answer and thinking, "I don't know." Then, he would shift his focus to one of the many other things fighting for his attention. This caused the decision process to drag out.

But with AI as his Thought Partner, Florian could maintain momentum, identify alternative solutions, pick the best option, and then have AI challenge his thinking to increase the odds of success. AI helped him collapse weeks of thinking into a simple decision in under thirty minutes. That was incredibly valuable.

The Power of Perspective

The path to becoming an AI-driven leader is not always easy. Remember that struggling is a sign of growth. With practice, you'll learn how to communicate with AI to get powerful results.

The key is your communication. This is not a new skill. But in the context of AI, it will separate those who merely dabble with AI and those who wield it to build a competitive advantage.

When you face roadblocks and find yourself struggling, remember, you are here because you have not yet learned the skill of communicating with AI. Focus on using better quality communication ingredients, and you will get better results in a short period of time. The key is to keep trying!

In the next chapter, we will explore five use cases you can apply today to supercharge your leadership.

Here's the 20% from This Chapter

1. Artificial intelligence (AI) is a technology that enables computers and machines to perform tasks that usually require human intelligence.
2. It works following an Input → Processing → Output → Learning framework.
3. What most people think of when it comes to AI is generative AI. Large language models (LLMs) are how people interact with generative AI. Examples are ChatGPT, Claude, Gemini, Perplexity, and AI Thought Partner.™
4. AI is a tool to achieve your goals, not the end goal.
5. These are simple ways you can use AI to increase your productivity:
    - Strategic Thinking
    - Decision-making
    - Content creation
    - Idea generation
    - Analysis (data, content, ideas)
    - Research
6. There are risks when it comes to AI. Understand them and know how to manage them.
    - **Job Displacement:** Every job will evolve because the skills applied and processes followed will change. Focus on what's within your control: learning skills that will be valuable in an AI-driven world.
    - **Biases:** AI models can inherit biases from the data they're

trained on, so it's crucial to approach AI-generated results with a critical eye and apply your human judgment.

- **Hallucinations:** AI may sometimes make things up. Always fact-check AI's responses and ask it to cite sources or explain its reasoning.
- **Privacy:** Public AI models can be trained on the data you input, so be cautious about sharing sensitive information. Consider using AI solutions with robust privacy and security features.
- **Relationships with Machines versus Humans:** As AI becomes increasingly engaging and empathetic, it's essential to remember that true fulfillment comes from real human connections.
- **Abdicating Thought Leadership:** Resist the temptation to outsource your thinking to AI entirely. Use it as your Thought Partner, but always maintain your role as the Thought Leader, providing context and judgment to shape the final output.

7. Master your communication with AI. The quality of your communication determines the quality of your results.

8. Focus on using high-quality prompt ingredients to boost your communication and your results:

   - **Describe the Task:** What do you want it to do for you?
   - **Give Context:** What does it need to know to complete the task?
   - **Assign a Persona:** What expertise do you want it to bring to the table?

- **Specify Requirements:** Is there anything specific you want it to do? Create a list or a table? Write in a certain tone?
- **Establish Limits:** What do you want it to avoid doing?
- **Explain Why:** This will help you understand the reasoning.
- **Ask AI to Interview You:** Let AI do the heavy lifting of pulling the information out of your head to accomplish the task.

9. My favorite prompt recipe for strategic thinking is CRIT™: Context - Role - Interview - Task. This will take your results to a new level.

10. The fastest way to gain competence with AI is to use it daily. Put a sticky note on your desk with the question "How can AI help me do this?" Try it, you will thank me later.

Ready to Put AI Into Action?

If you want to put these prompts into action right now, our AI Thought Partner™ has been trained on everything in this chapter, including CRIT™. You don't even need to write the prompt. Just scan the QR code below or visit AiLeadership.com and tell it what you're working on.

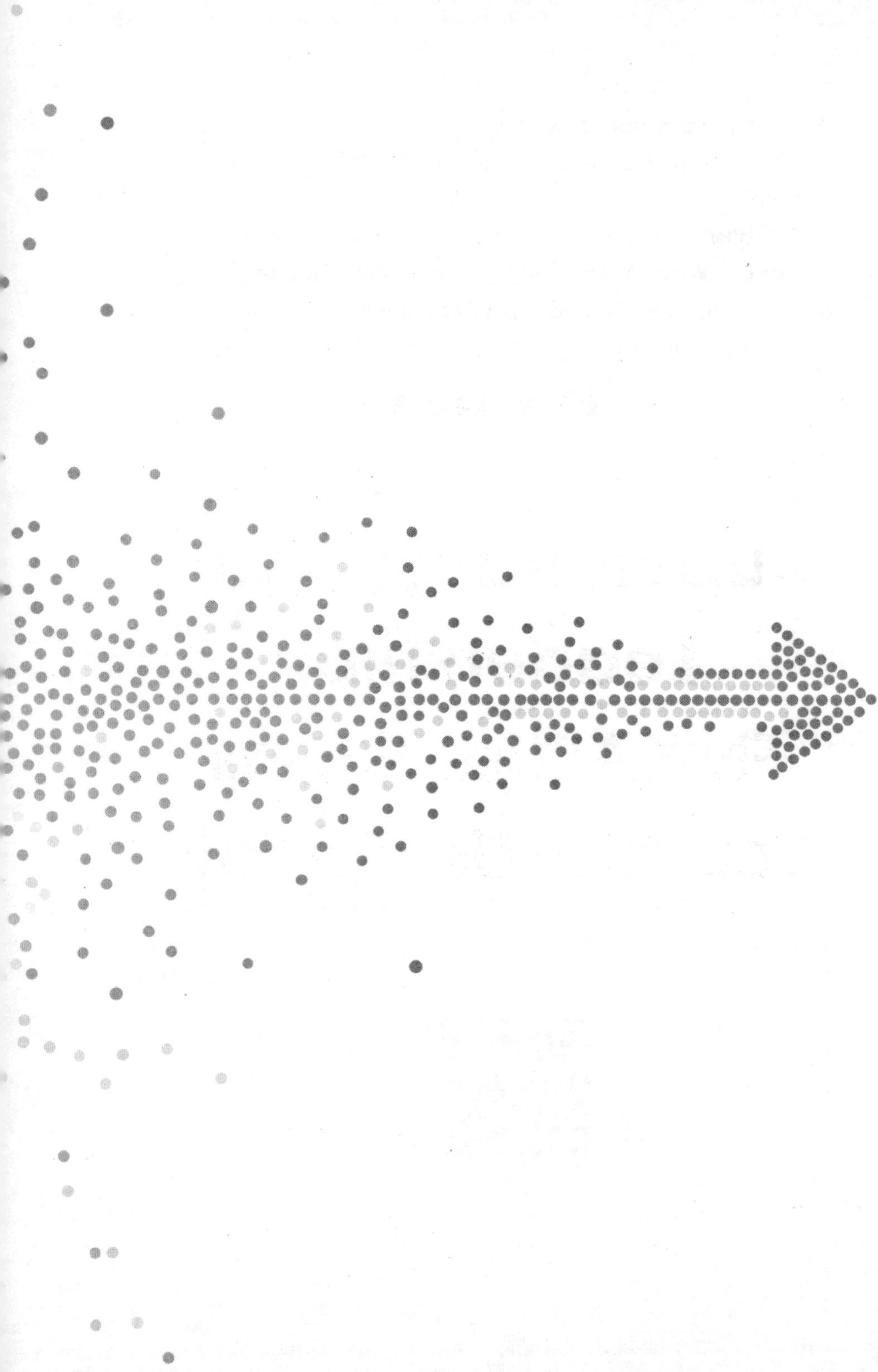

CHAPTER 5

Supercharge Your Leadership: Five AI Use Cases You Can Use Today

I'll never forget the lightbulb moment that changed my career. It was late 2022. I was hosting an off-site in India for the senior executives from our various operating companies to align on the future of leadership within the Jindal organization. On the first morning of the off-site, a colleague turned to me and asked "Have you heard of ChatGPT?" I shook my head. Then he leaned over and said, "Watch this."

He started typing a prompt, asking ChatGPT to help draft a communication for his team. He gave high-level bullets of what he wanted in the message, the tone he wanted to strike, and the psychology of what would resonate with his team. Then he submitted the prompt. I watched ChatGPT immediately generate the message based on his guidance. It was incredible and was the first time I saw AI turn a relatable moment into a remarkable experience. I got the sense that this would be a skill worth mastering.

As the day unfolded, the team and I talked about what the future of Jindal leadership might look like. A key issue that surfaced was employee productivity. With a workforce of over 100,000 people worldwide, we had implemented a system to help each employee prioritize their time each week. However, there was often misalignment between the individual actions and the broader organizational goals. Addressing this disconnect became a key priority I would champion.

After the off-site, I sat down for my routine strategic thinking time—a sacred, uninterrupted slot on my calendar—and my mind began to work over potential solutions. I scribbled the pivotal question at the top of my notepad:

How might we align the actions of our people with our organizational goals?

I spent the next few minutes jotting down potential answers. Then after reviewing my initial thoughts, I wrote down two more questions:

1. *What assumptions am I making right now?*
2. *What don't I see?*

As I reflected on these questions, a lightbulb moment struck again. My former mentor's advice comes to mind: "It's tough to read the label when you're inside the box." I was still confined by my own perspective. I need to think differently. That's when I recalled my colleague and ChatGPT.

"Up to that point, I'd asked the same question, 'How can I do this?' At that moment I found myself asking, 'How might AI help me do this?'"

Up to that point, I'd asked the same question, "How can ***I*** do this?" At that moment I found myself asking, "How might ***AI*** help me do this?" Feeling inspired by this new approach to strategic thinking, I crafted a prompt for AI:

> As the chief growth officer of a large organization, I've noticed a big challenge. Despite our growth and success, we're not reaching our full potential. This is because what people do on a weekly basis does not always align with driving progress on our organizational goals. This leads to wasted time, money, and resources.
>
> I want you to act as a strategic adviser with expertise in aligning a large workforce to help me come up with potential solutions. Here are three solutions I've come up with: (Then I listed those solutions). I would like you to identify alternative solutions that I have not thought of yet so I can have a comprehensive list to consider.
>
> Please structure your answer in order of priority, and explain why you are making each recommendation.

Instantly, the AI generated a list of innovative ways to align individual actions with organizational goals—and a few of those potential strategies were more creative and impactful than my initial ideas.

After discarding a few that seemed less valuable, I quickly realized that combining my human context with AI's processing power created a powerful synergy I could use to my advantage.

Feeling energized, I began drafting the business case for this initiative. Then it hit me again: I'm asking "How can *I* do this?" when I could be asking "How might *AI* help me do this?"

I opened a new dialogue with the AI:

> I need your help creating a business case for an initiative to increase the productivity of our employees across our organizations.
>
> For context, we are a large steel company with multiple operating companies across the globe.
>
> I want you to structure the business case around the following sections:
>
> 1. What we are trying to do and why it matters
> 2. How it will impact the organization
> 3. What the implementation plan looks like
> 4. What financial investment will be required and the roi
> 5. What the risks are and plans to mitigate them
> 6. What our next steps are
>
> Please interview me, asking me one question at a time to pull the necessary information out of my head, so you can then create a draft of this business case. Once you have enough information, generate the business case following the structure above.

With that, I hit enter and eagerly awaited the AI's response.

The AI began interviewing me, asking insightful questions that prompted deeper reflection on my part. The experience was remarkably humanlike, and time seemed to melt away as I engaged in the virtual dialogue. Suddenly, the AI generated a draft business case that not only articulated my thoughts clearly but also connected ideas I hadn't initially seen.

While the draft wasn't perfect, I was amazed by how quickly it got me to a solid draft. Instead of spending days creating it from scratch, I was able to delegate that phase to AI and make myself the editor. The entire process took less than thirty minutes—a stark contrast to the weeks it might have taken without AI assistance.

Get More Done in Less Time: The Five AI Use Cases You Can Use Today

In this chapter, I will show you the top five ways you can use AI to immediately boost your productivity. Here they are:

1. Strategic Thinking
2. Decision-making
3. Content creation
4. Idea generation
5. Analysis

Using AI for Strategic Thinking

AI can be a powerful Thought Partner, helping you think outside the box and generate fresh ideas. Like playing ping pong with a brilliant colleague, AI gives you the ability to communicate back and forth, challenges assumptions, offers new perspectives, and helps you develop better solutions faster. Here are three key personas AI can adopt to support and enhance your strategic thinking:

Persona 1: The Interviewer

The Interviewer acts like a skilled journalist, asking you smart questions to uncover great ideas you didn't know you had. When struggling to organize your thoughts, ask AI to interview you, posing one question at a time, to help accomplish a specific task.

> I am in the process of brainstorming ideas for a new product. I would like you to act as an expert interviewer with deep expertise in product positioning to help me come up with a concept for a product. I'd like you to do this by asking me one question at a time and responding based on my answers to help me clarify:
>
> 1. The needs of my customer.
> 2. The gaps that exist in the market today.
> 3. How this product might help us build a competitive advantage.
>
> Once you feel you have enough information, please generate some potential product ideas.

The Interviewer can also help you when hiring. It can help you write a clear job description as well as identify interview questions.

This is something one of our advisory clients, Tanner Luster, CEO of Primally Pure, experienced firsthand while leading his amazing clean skincare company. He used AI to prepare for a crucial director-level interview. He uploaded the job description to AI, which was able to see that there were two key priorities for this role: building and leading a team, and focusing on data-driven e-commerce. AI generated relevant questions Tanner could ask the candidates in those areas. While Tanner could have come up with these questions himself, it would have taken at least thirty minutes of uninterrupted thinking time. AI did this in under one minute, saving Tanner time and enhancing interview quality.

Persona 2: The Communicator

The Communicator is a super-smart assistant that turns complex ideas into simple, powerful messages. It organizes your thoughts and determines the best way to share ideas so everyone—from your team to investors—really understands.

> We are launching a new product (describe the product). Act as The Communicator to help me craft a compelling pitch that highlights our product's unique features. Interview me by asking one question at a time. Once you have enough information, craft the pitch.

In times of crisis, the Communicator can help develop transparent messages that address issues directly, reassure stakeholders, and outline clear resolutions.

The Communicator can also assist in creating high-quality performance reviews for your people. While every company does them, not all leaders do them well. AI can be a powerful Thought Partner here by pulling the valuable insights out of your head and structuring them in a clear message that will resonate with your direct reports.

This is something Adria Campbell got to experience firsthand as chief revenue officer of MALK Organics, the leading premium plant-based milk company. I was brought in to help the executive team become AI-driven leaders. She first asked it to act as the Interviewer, where the AI asked her questions for about five minutes. Once the AI had enough information on the direct report, it became the Communicator and generated the performance review and the exact email she could send. Was it perfect? No, but it was 90% there. Adria made a few final touches, and it was done.

When I asked her how using AI differed from doing it herself, Adria said it was significantly easier having AI as her Thought Partner. It allowed her to answer questions while AI structured her thoughts into a concise message. She got the review done faster and felt the quality was higher.

This is one use case where I consistently see AI enhancing you, not replacing you. You cannot drive growth without your people. Giving them high-quality feedback raises their performance, which accelerates growth. Try this. You will thank me later.

Persona 3: The Challenger

One of the most valuable roles AI can play in strategic thinking is that of the Challenger. In this capacity, AI acts as an impartial judge, questioning your assumptions, poking holes in your arguments, and pushing you to consider alternative perspectives. By pressure testing your ideas, the Challenger helps you identify blind spots, anticipate potential objections, and strengthen your strategies.

Imagine you're preparing to present a new initiative to your board of directors. You've poured countless hours into crafting the perfect plan, and you're convinced it's the best way forward. But before you step into the boardroom, you decide to run your proposal by the Challenger.

You put your plan into AI, along with any relevant context and data (assuming AI meets your security needs). Then, you ask the Challenger to review your plan as if it were a skeptical board member, looking for any weaknesses or areas of concern. AI analyzes your plan from multiple angles, harnessing its processing power to scan all the data it's been trained on to identify potential risks and drawbacks that you may have overlooked.

Here are questions the Challenger gave me when I did this with our AI Thought Partner™:

1. How does this initiative align with your company's long-term strategic goals?
2. What assumptions are you making about market demand, and how have you validated them?
3. What is the potential impact on your cash flow and profitability?
4. What are the key risks associated with this plan, and how will you mitigate them?

Pretty good, right?

As you work through the Challenger's questions and feedback, you're forced to confront the vulnerabilities in your proposal. You might realize that you need to gather more data to support your assumptions or that you need to think deeper about how to mitigate risk. By addressing these issues proactively, you can refine your plan and increase your chances of success when you do present it to the board.

Of course, it's important to remember that the Challenger is a tool, not a decision-maker. Its role is to enhance your thinking, not to replace it. As Thought Leader, it's up to you to weigh the Challenger's output against your own judgment and expertise and make the final call on how to proceed.

By embracing AI as your Thought Partner, you can elevate your thinking, make more informed decisions, and ultimately drive growth of your company. So the next time you're mentally wrestling with a challenge, **instead of asking, "How might I solve this?" ask, "How might AI help me solve this?"** You will be surprised how much it can sharpen your thinking and improve your results.

If you want to try using the Interviewer, the Communicator, or the Challenger, our AI Thought Partner™ has been trained on these personas. Just ask it to adopt one of those personas, and it will help you get started. Scan the QR code or visit AiLeadership.com.

Using AI to make Better Decisions

Your decisions can make or break your business. As an AI-driven leader, one of your primary goals is to make better, faster decisions that drive sustainable business growth. This is not easy. You're often faced with incomplete or contradictory data, competing priorities, and tight timelines, all of which can lead to analysis paralysis or suboptimal choices.

This is where AI can be a valuable partner to you. It can transform the way you make decisions in a fraction of the time. (We will cover this in detail in chapter 9.)

For example, let's say you're considering whether to acquire a smaller competitor to expand your market share. Traditionally, this decision would require a significant amount of time for research, financial modeling, and debate among your leadership team. But with AI, you can streamline this process dramatically.

You can feed AI data on the target company's financials, customer base, product offerings, and market. The AI can then analyze this data in a matter of seconds and spot potential patterns around key risks and opportunities.

Armed with these insights, you can have a more informed and productive discussion with your team, focusing on the most critical issues and trade-offs, rather than getting bogged down in data collection and analysis. You can also use the AI to pressure test your assumptions and challenge your biases, ensuring that you're making the best possible decision based on the available evidence.

Of course, AI is not a substitute for your human judgment and expertise. It's still up to you, as a leader, to weigh the AI's recommendations against your own experience and intuition. You will want to consider factors that may not be captured in the data, such as company culture, the expectations of stakeholders, and your long-term goals.

By leveraging AI as your Thought Partner, you can make more informed, data-driven decisions in a fraction of the time. This frees you up to focus on higher-level strategic thinking and leadership.

"By leveraging AI as your Thought Partner, you can make more informed, data-driven decisions in a fraction of the time. This frees you up to focus on higher-level strategic thinking and leadership."

Using AI for Content Creation

AI can significantly streamline content creation, from emails to articles to proposals, by helping you transform thoughts into written words. This includes writing material directly or structuring it to fit a specific tone. A leader I interviewed shared an insightful experience: after conducting a tough performance review, he wrote a follow-up email that initially seemed too harsh. He turned to AI for help:

> I just concluded a performance review with an employee. After writing the follow-up email, I realized it comes off as too harsh. I need it rewritten to be clear on expectations and maintain firm performance standards but also be empathetic and softer so the employee receives it well. Below is the original email; please regenerate it based on this description.

The AI then restructured the email in the desired tone. After reviewing and making a few final adjustments, the leader sent the email, which was well received by the employee.

When using AI for content creation, it's crucial to understand the two roles at play: the Thought Leader and the Thought Partner. Many users mistakenly expect AI to lead the creative process. They might ask AI to write an email or blog post and simply copy and paste the generated content without reviewing it to ensure it meets their standards. This is not how you will get value from AI. It will only lead to mediocre work.

Remember, AI is a prediction machine. The content it will generate might be 50% to 60% of where you need it to be. That's okay. Then you step in as the Thought Leader to apply your judgment and experience to ensure it is delivering the right message in the right way. Do not abdicate your responsibility as the Thought Leader.

Using AI for Idea Generation

Your ability to generate fresh, innovative ideas is crucial to driving growth. However, if you're not naturally gifted with an overflowing well of creativity, you may find yourself settling for *the first idea* that comes to mind rather than searching for *the best idea*. This is where AI can be invaluable as your Thought Partner. Instead of hitting a mental wall and thinking, "I don't know," which disrupts your momentum, you can turn to AI for help.

Here are three key ways AI can help with idea generation:

1. Generating additional ideas to expand your initial list of solutions.
2. Identifying non-obvious ideas to challenge your biases and assumptions.
3. Narrowing down a broad list of ideas to a shortlist for further consideration.

For example, one CEO we advise wanted to double his company's revenue in the next twenty-four months. This is a private company working toward an exit, so I will keep them anonymous for this example. The problem was, the team was struggling to identify a clear path to delivering this result. I showed the CEO how to harness AI as his Thought Partner to help generate potential solutions.

> Our goal is to double revenue in the next twenty-four months to become an attractive acquisition target. Attached is our strategic plan. I want you to act as a strategic growth expert by helping me identify non-obvious alternatives we could consider to drive this growth. You can ask me up to five questions to gather what you need about my business. Once you have sufficient context, give me your recommendations listed in order of priority and explain why you are making each recommendation.

AI conducted a short interview of the CEO, gathering context about the business and the industry and then about the specific ways he was looking at driving growth. Once it had enough information, it generated a list of five alternative growth strategies. The CEO reviewed the list. Three were okay, and one was garbage, but one surprised him. It was a fantastic idea they should have recognized from the beginning but had overlooked. Ding! He had the lightbulb moment.

Using AI for Analysis (Data, Content, Ideas)

AI can transform how you analyze data, significantly enhancing your strategic capabilities. Before I used AI, I remember painstakingly reviewing hundreds of customer reviews in a spreadsheet, trying to identify patterns based on what caught my attention. With AI, you can simply upload a spreadsheet and talk to it like a colleague. AI can write code to sift through the data and generate valuable insights on the spot. (We'll explore this more thoroughly in chapter 7.)

AI can also evaluate the quality of your content. I met with the head of investor relations for a growth company in the enterprise software space. He had prepared his remarks for an upcoming investor meeting but felt uneasy. He said, "We had a good quarter. The business is doing great, but there are certain metrics that don't look amazing, and I'm concerned people will focus on those and lose sight of how well the company is really doing."

I told him this was a perfect use for AI to help him analyze his content and enhance it to deliver the desired outcome. I had him open AI, upload the statement he had drafted, and explain to AI exactly what he had explained to me. I waited while he typed the prompt. Then I gave him one final piece to include:

> Acting as an investor, analyze this communication and outline:
>
> 1. Where you think the company is doing well.
> 2. Where you might have concerns.
>
> Based on that, please regenerate the message to minimize concerns. Avoid deviating from my core content. Everything stated must be truthful. I just want to minimize the downside.

AI instantly gave an analysis as directed and then offered a simple solution on how to reframe certain metrics to minimize the data being misinterpreted.

I could see the weight being lifted off this person's shoulders as he read this. He incorporated the changes, and the meeting went well.

Finally, AI can analyze your ideas. As I have been building AI Leadership, I regularly have ideas about the business. To enhance my thinking, I turn to AI to analyze the idea as my customer:

> I want you to act as an ambitious non-technical executive of a growth company. Here is an idea I have for a product offering: (then I describe the product). Here's the problem I believe it solves and the benefits it will bring. My goal is that you will see this solution and think, "This is exactly what I need!" Your goal is to tell me what you like about my idea, what you do not like, and the top changes I should consider making and explain why they are important to you.

Every time I do this, AI spots something I have overlooked. In every single situation, I have improved my thinking with this use case. Give it a try. You will thank me later.

Big changes start with small actions. My guidance to you is to start trying these five use cases and see if you can have lightbulb moments. They have the power to transform your productivity and decision-making. If you do not get valuable results at first, remember that the issue may not be AI; it might be your communication. Focus on using quality ingredients and stick with it. Over time, you'll build momentum, which will lead to harnessing AI in more use cases, which will accelerate your progress, and eventually, you will expand what's possible. Along the way, remember you are the Thought Leader, guiding AI as your Thought Partner. Stay in the driver's seat!

In the next chapter, I'll show you the high price of asking the wrong questions, and how you can use AI to overcome your biases and assumptions.

Here's the 20% from This Chapter

1. AI can redefine your strategic thinking and transform your decision-making. This can help you drive accelerated growth.

2. AI can bring value to you through the following use cases:

    - Strategic thinking
    - Decision-making
    - Content creation
    - Idea generation
    - Analysis (data, content, ideas)

3. When asking AI to act as your Thought Partner, consider having it play these three roles:

    - **The Interviewer:** Ask AI to interview you to gather the information in your head and help you clarify your thinking.
    - **The Communicator:** Engage AI to turn complex ideas into simple, powerful messages.
    - **The Challenger:** Ask AI to challenge your thinking so you overcome your biases and assumptions.

4. Here are additional ways AI can enhance your strategic thinking:

    - **Providing Faster and More Accurate Data Analysis:** With AI, you collapse the time it takes to turn data into decisions. (We will cover this in more detail in Chapter 7.)
    - **Generating "Outside the Box" Ideas:** Your perspective is limited. Instead of settling for *an* answer, engage AI to surface *the best* answer.
    - **Providing Logic and Reasoning:** AI can offer logic and

reasoning to ideas, helping you narrow your focus and refine your strategies.

- **Simulating Outcomes:** Simulate potential outcomes of decisions so you can understand how things might play out and spot potential blind spots.
- **Adopting Personas for Feedback:** Have AI adopt the persona of a key customer or internal stakeholder and give you feedback from their perspective. This helps you see things from different viewpoints and improve your thinking.

CHAPTER 6

The High Price of The Wrong Questions: Using AI to Overcome Biases and Assumptions

Great leaders aren't the ones with all the answers. They're the ones who ask the right questions. Unfortunately, many leaders ask the wrong ones when it comes to strategic thinking and decision-making. This leads their teams astray, wasting tremendous amounts of time and money. This all stems from unchallenged biases and assumptions. Fortunately, AI can help, providing better information for faster, smarter decisions.

Take Keith Cunningham's experience as a cautionary tale. Keith J. Cunningham, an American entrepreneur and author of *The Road Less Stupid*, is known for his presentations at Tony Robbins's business mastery events and as the real "Rich Dad" in Robert Kiyosaki's *Rich Dad, Poor Dad*.

In the 1980s, Keith's real estate investments in the southwestern US made him a fortune, with assets worth two to three times his debt. Confident in his success, Keith focused on questions like, "How can we acquire more real estate?" and "How can we access more capital?" But these were the wrong questions.

In 1989, the real estate market collapsed. Keith's assets plunged to just 20% of their original value, while his debt remained unchanged. His once cash-flowing empire couldn't even cover taxes, insurance, and maintenance fees. Keith recounts in *The Road Less Stupid*, "We had no cash or cash flow. And we all had personal liability that far exceeded the market value of our assets. We were stone cold broke with no possibility of recovery. The hole was too deep."

From my conversations with Keith, one thing stood out: this catastrophic loss occurred because he was asking the wrong questions, costing him over $100 million. Keith put it best in our interview:

"At university, just like life, there are courses. Every single course has tuition. I took a course in the University of Life, and the tuition was $100 million. Not very many people get to take this course." As he and I chatted, he told me it was not about how much the course cost but about whether it was worth the investment. In Keith's case, what he learned was worth every penny.

Keith noted in his book, "The key to getting rich and staying that way is to avoid doing stupid things. I don't need to do more smart things; I just need to stop doing a few dumb things. I need to avoid making emotional decisions and swinging at bad pitches. I need to think." This lesson helped him claw his way out of that $100 million hole, ultimately building beyond his previous success and staying there.

> **"Great leaders aren't the ones with all the answers. They're the ones who ask the right questions."**

The Consequences of Asking the Wrong Questions

Asking the wrong questions can create huge problems and cost you lots of money—especially when you're not aware that you're asking them. In Keith's case, the wrong questions cost him over $100 million. Biases and assumptions in leadership are invisible anchors, slowing even the strongest ships. Unfortunately, we're so used to the drag that we don't notice the disadvantage we're working with. Here's how these biases creep into decision-making:

Narrowing Perspectives: Imagine peering through a telescope but seeing only a tiny, fog-covered view. Biases obscure critical perspectives, preventing you from recognizing new opportunities or warnings that could be vital.

Reinforcing the Status Quo: Like navigating a new city with an old, familiar map, biases lead leaders to stick with outdated strategies.

They fail to realize that the same old approaches won't work in new situations, causing them to miss crucial trends and technologies.

Throwing Good Money After Bad: Ever seen a kid pouring more and more quarters into a claw machine that just won't give up a prize? That's the sunk cost fallacy. Leaders sometimes keep throwing resources into failing projects because they've already invested so much, even when it's clear that stopping might be the smarter choice.

Ron Johnson's tenure at JCPenney is a textbook case of biases and assumptions leading to disaster. When he took over as CEO in 2011, he believed he could replicate his Apple success. After all, he had masterminded Apple's revolutionary retail strategy, transforming stores into experiential hubs that drove sales and loyalty.

Johnson firmly believed that the strategies that had worked so well at Apple could be seamlessly applied to revitalize the struggling JCPenney brand. But Johnson underestimated the differences between the companies.

At Apple, Johnson had implemented an "everyday low pricing" model, eliminating discounts and coupons. He envisioned the same approach at JCPenney, scrapping "dubious pricing policies" for "fair and square" pricing. But he overlooked that JCPenney shoppers expected the constant promotions and discounts integral to the brand's identity.

Similarly, Johnson planned to change JCPenney stores into more interactive spaces, like Apple's stores. But he didn't consider that what worked for tech-savvy Apple enthusiasts wouldn't resonate with JCPenney's traditional, price-conscious shoppers.

Johnson also assumed that introducing trendier brands would revive the company. However, this move alienated loyal customers, leaving them confused and disoriented by the sudden changes.

Ultimately, Ron Johnson's biases and assumptions blinded him to the reality that JCPenney's customers were not Apple's customers. Sales plummeted, and its stock price plunged.

Johnson's story is a wake-up call, reminding us that strategic thinking must be rooted in a deep understanding of reality. We can't just rely on assumptions based on past wins. As leaders, we have to be on constant lookout for our own biases and assumptions. Only then can we make great decisions that drive sustainable growth.

Recognizing and Overcoming Cognitive Biases in Leadership

As an AI-driven leader, it's crucial to understand how our minds can sometimes steer us wrong. Cognitive biases, those sneaky mental shortcuts, can subtly influence our decision-making without us even realizing it. Let's unpack some common biases that can trip up your leadership effectiveness and explore how to outsmart them.

CONFIRMATION BIAS: THE "YES MAN" IN YOUR MIND

Think of confirmation bias as that little voice in your head that's always cheering, "Yes!" to your ideas but conveniently ignores anything that challenges them. This bias makes us seek out information that supports what we already believe and turn a blind eye to what doesn't fit. It can show up like this:

- **Echo Chamber:** You only listen to team members who agree with your strategy, missing critical insights from the dissenters.
- **Selective Hearing:** You ignore data that contradicts your grand plans for a new product launch, leading to a surprise flop.

To combat this, actively seek out diverse opinions and challenge your own assumptions. This prevents groupthink and ensures your strategies are well rounded and rock solid.

ANCHORING BIAS: FIRST IMPRESSIONS STICK

Anchoring bias happens when we rely too heavily on the first piece of information we get (the "anchor") and let it shape our decisions way more than it should. For example:

- **Price Anchoring:** If the first budget estimate you hear is sky high, all the numbers after that might seem reasonable in comparison, even if they're also inflated.
- **Initial Impressions:** Early success with a marketing strategy might anchor your expectations, causing you to miss subtle shifts in consumer behavior that are screaming, "Time for a change!"

Avoid getting anchored by gathering tons of information before you make big decisions. Revisit your initial assumptions regularly, and adjust based on the latest data, not just your first impressions.

SUNK COST FALLACY: THROWING GOOD MONEY AFTER BAD

The sunk cost fallacy makes us toss good resources after bad ones, just because we've already invested so much. Here's how it might look:

- **Failing Projects:** You keep pouring money into a project that's clearly tanking simply because you've already sunk a fortune into it.
- **Past Decisions:** You stick with a subpar supplier because you've worked with the supplier for years and it feels easier than making a switch.

To break free from this fallacy, focus on future potential, not past costs. Regularly review your investments, and be ready to cut your losses if the future benefits don't justify further spending. This ensures you're always chasing new opportunities, not chained to past decisions.

Harness the power of AI to help you spot and overcome these

cognitive biases. Prompt AI to play the role of the Challenger, challenging your assumptions and calling out potential biases in your thinking. By combining your human context with AI processing power, you will elevate your strategic thinking and make faster, smarter decisions that will drive your organization forward.

Techniques for Questioning Assumptions with AI

While AI can be a powerful Thought Partner, it needs careful prompting. Otherwise, it can amplify biases and assumptions instead of challenging them. Joe Riesberg, the CIO of EMC Insurance, knows this firsthand. He's been instrumental in integrating AI at EMC, a key provider of property and casualty insurance across the US.

During our chat, Joe shared how EMC participated in a study featured in the March-April 2024 *Harvard Business Review*. EMC wanted to see if AI could help its agents find innovative ways to optimize interactions and boost customer service. The team was split into two groups: one using AI, the other working without it. Those using AI fed documents about the company and its services into the system and then tasked their agents with using AI to find the most creative answers to achieve the goal.

In the HBR article, Joe was asked, "Were you surprised by the results?"

He shared, "I was! When I left work that day, I thought that the quality, quantity, and depth of the answers ChatGPT had given my employees on the experimental team were really powerful—surely better than the human-only answers. Turns out I was wrong!"

The issue was that the agents came up with initial ideas and asked AI to make them better. This was not the goal. The goal was to come up with the most creative ideas to optimize interactions and boost customer service. But the way the agents communicated with AI caused it to stay within the boundaries of enhancing the existing ideas rather than getting outside the box and generating the most creative solutions. Instead of challenging their biases, AI amplified them.

Joe emphasized that people are often unaware of their biases and assumptions. If you ask AI to build on flawed foundations, it will simply magnify the mistakes. Instead, the team could have prompted AI more effectively, saying, "I'm an agent with EMC Insurance. Here are five solutions I've come up with. Please identify alternative solutions you think would be more creative."

If the agents had used this prompt, AI would have been encouraged to go outside the box rather than work within it. With this lesson, Joe is now able to lead his people to better harness AI to make better decisions.

It's vital that we, as AI-driven leaders, raise awareness of our biases and assumptions and teach our teams to prompt AI in ways that challenge those biases instead of reinforcing them. Here are additional strategies you can use.

Data-Driven Insights: AI's Unbiased Lens

AI is a data-crunching powerhouse, able to analyze massive datasets and uncover hidden gems of insight that might slip past your human analysts. This can help you to rethink long-held beliefs and assumptions. With this at your fingertips, you can make faster, smarter decisions.

> We are a steel manufacturing company. Attached is our order book history for the last three years showing production by product by plant. I've also attached our sales projections for this upcoming year showing the same. This includes

> assumptions we have made on what production might look like by product at each plant. Acting as the Analyst, please review the data to identify underlying trends to validate or challenge our assumptions.

SCENARIO SIMULATION: AI'S CRYSTAL BALL

AI is like a crystal ball for your business, able to simulate how things might play out depending on different factors. You can ask it to simulate everything from economic outcomes to competitive responses to how customers or internal stakeholders might respond. This can be a very valuable tool, as one company I advise found out.

This consumer packaged goods company, which will remain anonymous, sells their products in grocery stores across the US, including Whole Foods. They had a meeting scheduled with Jason Buechel, the CEO of Whole Foods, to discuss expanding their partnership. The team put together a simple two-page presentation to justify the expansion.

A week before the meeting, the CEO of the consumer packaged goods company asked me, "Can AI help us here?"

"Well," I asked him, "how clear are you on what matters to Whole Foods in a partnership, and how well does your presentation align with what they care about?" The CEO had solid answers to these questions; however, he wanted to test his assumption.

I fired up AI and wrote the following prompt:

> I am an executive with a consumer packaged goods company. We have a meeting coming up with the CEO of Whole Foods. Our goal is to gain strategic alignment as a preferred partner.
>
> Your role is to research Jason Buechel, the CEO, and identify what matters most to him in a partnership.

Then I hit enter.

Instantly, AI generated a response outlining six different priorities Jason would consider, each backed by a reference link so we could check if this was fact or a hallucination. Then I wrote the following prompt:

> Now act as Jason Buechel, the Whole Foods CEO, in reviewing the attached presentation against the six priorities you've outlined.
>
> Please structure your response highlighting:
>
> 1. The strengths of our presentation.
> 2. What we are missing.
> 3. What we can do to improve.

The AI quickly outlined the strengths of the existing presentation, and then it delivered something that left the CEO speechless:

> Whole Foods cares about ethical sourcing and fair trade. These are strengths of your brand; however, there is no information on your presentation highlighting these points. Here is what you might say and where you can include it in your presentation.

AI suggested content to be included and outlined exactly where to place it. The CEO updated the deck immediately to account for these new insights.

Before using AI, the CEO felt confident their presentation was a 10/10. However, by harnessing AI to simulate the customer, we were able to identify key gaps that mattered to Whole Foods. The total time investment? Less than fifteen minutes.

DEVIL'S ADVOCATE: AI'S CONTRARIAN VOICE

Every leader needs a devil's advocate to challenge assumptions and poke holes in plans. AI can play this role to perfection. By generating counterarguments and alternative perspectives, it can test the strength of your strategies and your decisions.

> Attached is our strategic plan for the next fiscal year. Acting as the Devil's Advocate, review our plan and ask critical questions that could expose flaws in the plan's ability to achieve our overall goal. Please prepare a detailed report evaluating the strengths and weaknesses of our strategy, and offer recommendations to improve.

PREMORTEMS AND POSTMORTEMS: AI'S TIME MACHINE

Evaluating risk isn't just about external forces. AI-driven leaders also use AI to assess internal risks. One of the companies we advise, which will remain anonymous, exemplifies this. Despite their success, they faced a challenge: an activist board deeply involved in operations and eager to find flaws in every decision. Each board meeting was a battle, with members often being confrontational.

We introduced AI to help. The executive team used AI to interview them to understand the personality of each board member on a deep level and then generate detailed profiles. We then created a personalized AI model, uploaded the board profiles, and trained the AI model to simulate board member behavior. With this, we now had a tool for AI-driven premortems and postmortems.

Here's how it worked: before each board meeting, the team would upload the board deck and ask AI to simulate potential reactions. In a test with a past deck, AI predicted:

> On slide 8, Susan will get distracted by the granularity of the details. This will lead to a 30-minute detour that derails your entire agenda. Instead of all the details, say these three things—because they're what she cares about most.

The CEO looked at me and said, "This is exactly what happened. For another meeting, we uploaded the deck, and AI said:

> Susan will want to see the unit-level economics of club versus retail pricing. Providing this detail will gain her trust.

The CEO said, "She absolutely will!" They updated the deck immediately, avoiding a potential landmine. After each meeting, we uploaded the transcript from the real meeting to AI, which compared its predictions with the actual responses and updated each personality profile. This continuous learning made the AI board better at helping the executive team prepare for future meetings.

It's tough to read the label when you're inside the box. Sometimes, you are so close to the business that you can lose sight of important information in your decision. AI's ability to simulate potential outcomes makes it an invaluable tool for conducting premortems. It allows you to proactively identify and address potential points of failure before they happen. When it comes to postmortems, AI can help analyze successes and failures, pinpointing faulty assumptions and biases that led to less-than-stellar outcomes. This will make you a better strategic planner and decision-maker.

By weaving AI into these key aspects of strategic thinking, you can ensure your decisions are data-driven, comprehensive, and future-focused. Stay in the driver's seat and allow AI to enhance your judgment.

However, having the right tools is only part of the equation. The questions you ask can significantly impact your results.

The Power of Asking the Right Questions

In my time as an executive coach, advisor, and executive, I've learned that the questions I ask can shape how people see the world. It's a superpower when used to help others. I think of one CEO I worked with. Let's call him Brian. Brian had just stepped into the top job at a company in turnaround mode. Pressure was high, and cash was low. The constant drumbeat was: "Do more with less."

While Brian stepped in with an initial plan, the board quickly became overly involved, constantly challenging him and telling him he needed to be running in a different direction.

In one of my conversations with Brian, he said, "Let me just get through my first ninety days to get my sea legs. Let me build some credibility with the board, and then I'll start asserting myself."

I wondered what questions Brian was asking himself at that moment. What assumptions might be steering him wrong? I asked. He said, "I'm trying to figure out how to build enough rapport and trust with the board so they'll let me do what I want." It seemed logical to him, but it was the wrong question.

I drew a car on a piece of paper, with a driver's seat, passenger seat, and trunk. I asked, "What seat are you in right now? Are you in the driver's seat? Or are you in the passenger seat, watching the board drive? Or have you locked yourself in the trunk, thinking nothing can change?" He realized he was in the passenger seat, with the board at the wheel. I said, "Exactly. Now, imagine the best version of yourself as CEO. Where would that version

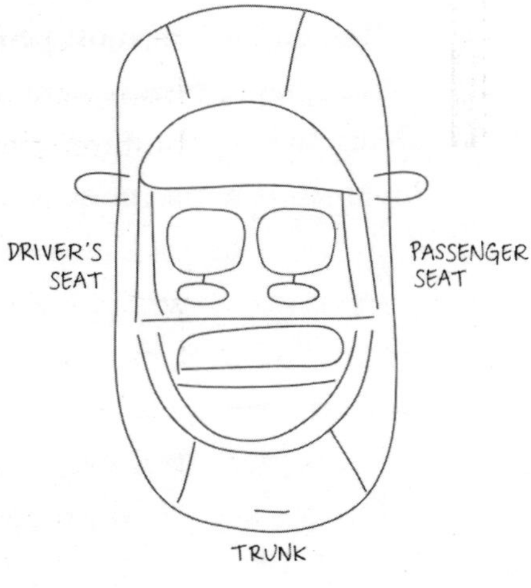

sit?" He said the driver's seat. I asked, "What questions would that version of you be asking?"

Brian took a deep breath and sighed. "Great question." We sat in silence as he processed. Then he said, "I'd be asking myself, 'What are the most important things we need to accomplish in the first ninety days to drive progress toward our most critical goals while earning the board's trust?'" It was a fantastic question. It focused on the goal. It was simple and clear, and it provoked deeper thinking.

As Brian explored his answers, he broke free from his initial biases and assumptions. He realized he needed a different conversation with the board. There was misalignment on what *they* thought he should do, what *he* thought he should do, and who was *really* in charge. Brian had the meeting, got alignment, and executed.

As you lead your teams into the AI era, your ability to ask great questions will be a crucial skill. It not only enhances your thinking but breaks you out of biases and assumptions that can lead you astray. In the old way of working, most knowledge workers were operational, their days filled with tasks. But as we move forward, the value of the human knowledge worker will be strategic not operational. Our people need to focus less on *doing* and more on *thinking*, building a competitive advantage in the long term through the actions they take in the short term.

The problem is, most people have not been taught to think strategically from our time in school. Throughout college, we were rated on our ability to have the *right* answer, not on our ability to think and search for answers to bigger questions. This starts by asking great questions.

Characteristics of Great Questions

Great questions share three key characteristics:

1. They are aligned with your goals or the problem.
2. They are simple and clear.
3. They provoke deeper thinking.

On the other hand, poor-quality questions can derail your strategic efforts. A poor-quality question is either **too narrow (missing the bigger picture) or too broad (lacking focus).**

Poor-quality questions **are leading:** they presume a certain answer or a bias that skews the conversation or decision-making process.

Poor-quality questions **do not directly relate to the goals** of the organization. As a result, they can divert valuable focus away from what matters most.

Finally, poor-quality questions **fail to challenge assumptions.** Questions that don't challenge underlying assumptions and the status quo can result in stagnation and missed opportunities for innovation.

Conversely, a great question is focused on the goals or key problems that are preventing progress. It should always move the needle closer to achieving these targets. A great question is clear and concise, and it avoids ambiguity. Everyone involved understands what's being asked without needing extensive clarification. And it should provoke deeper thinking.

"I've learned that the questions I ask can shape how people see the world. It's a superpower when used to help others."

My Journey to Thinking Strategically and Asking Great Questions

November 1, 2015, was my first day starting the company behind *The ONE Thing*. Gary Keller had a surprising welcome for me: "Welcome to Austin. Good luck—you're going to need it," he said.

My response? "Hi. Thanks! Why?"

He looked at me and said, "Your biggest problem is that you're going to want to make me your product. You're going to want to put me on stage or in the podcast. Geoff, do you know what the best part about your job is? That it's *your* job. And if you try to give me pieces of your job, you will no longer have one." While I was surprised by the directness, this was a gift. On day 1, Gary set a very clear standard: if I needed him, then he didn't need me. So I needed to be able to succeed without him.

Jay later explained that his job as a leader was to teach me how to think so I could get what I needed independently. This took a little time to sink in. All my work experience had trained me to go to my boss for direction and to execute from there. I had been taught to think like an industrial worker. Gary and Jay were setting a clear boundary on day 1. I had to own 100% of my job—including strategic thinking! They wouldn't give me answers but would ask great questions so I could discover the right answers myself. What I didn't realize was that over the next several weeks, I would experience firsthand how transformative great questions could be.

The next week, I walked into Jay's office with a question. He looked at me and said, "Geoff, my job as a leader is to teach you how to think. What do you think the answer is?" While this was such a simple question, it was a great one. It was aligned with the goal of teaching me how to think. It was simple and clear, and it provoked deeper thinking.

I thought about it and gave him my answer. He replied, "That's exactly what I would have said, but now you own it."

"It's tough to read the label when you're inside the box. Sometimes, you are so close to the business that you can lose sight of important information in your decision."

The following week, I had another question. Jay asked, "Geoff, my job is to teach you how to think. What do you think you should do?" I gave him my answer. This time, he said, "That's one way you could do it. What might some alternative solutions be?" It happened again! Such a simple question that was aligned with his goal of teaching me how to think, and it provoked deeper thinking. It was like he was guiding me at the bowling alley, acting as bumper rails to prevent my ideas from going off track. I gave him a revised recommendation, and he agreed with it.

By the third week, I walked into his office with a question and said, "I know. I know. Your job is to teach me how to think. Here's the situation. Here's what I think we should do. Coach me on that."

This experience created a shift in my identity as a leader. I began shifting from an industrial way of working, where my boss told me what to do, to a strategic way of working, where I stayed in the driver's seat and did my own thinking. I also realized that mastering the skill of asking great questions is invaluable. Ever since, I have pursued mastery in asking questions that are focused on the goal, clear and simple, and provoke deeper thinking. Ultimately, this became the foundation of our AI Thought Partner™—an AI-driven strategy execution system designed to ask the right questions so leadership teams can think more clearly, align faster, make better decisions, and turn strategy into value in a fraction of the time.

The questions you ask yourself determine your future; they guide your focus, which guides your actions and ultimately your results. Becoming an AI-driven leader means shifting from playing at a tactical level to leading with strategic clarity. **Your ability to ask the**

right questions is a valuable skill. It will elevate your leadership by helping you overcome biases and assumptions, drive greater growth, and unlock new levels of value as you use AI as your Thought Partner.

How do you know if you're asking the right questions? Here's a simple checklist:

- Is your question aligned with your goals or solving the right problems?
- Is it simple and clear?
- Does it provoke deeper thinking?

If you can say yes to these three questions, then you are on the right track. If not, reword your question until you can. If you need help, turn to AI. Give it your initial question, and then give it the checklist above and ask it to generate alternative questions for you to consider. Once you have your question, go search for the answer!

Finally, I challenge you to ask questions that are big. The purpose of a goal is to inform who you can become. If you ask small questions constricted by what you think you can do or the resources you currently have, then you'll never play at a bigger level. Ask questions that are so big they challenge you to ask who you can become to get to that level. The journey of becoming is where your growth lives.

In the next chapter, I'll show you how you can collapse the time to turn data into decisions.

*If you want to see how AI can help you align faster, execute better, and drive value in a fraction of the time, visit AiLeadership.com

Here's the 20% from This Chapter

1. The questions you ask shape your future. Asking the wrong questions can cost you millions of dollars. Make sure you are asking the right ones.
2. A great question:
   - Is aligned with your goals
   - Is simple and clear
   - Provokes deeper thinking
3. Mastering asking great questions is a skill that will serve you no matter where you go. It will elevate your leadership, drive growth, and unlock value with AI as your Thought Partner.
4. We all have biases and assumptions that can lead us astray. To elevate your thinking, challenge them so you make decisions with clarity.
5. AI can challenge your biases or enhance them. The difference is how you direct it as the Thought Leader. Ask it to challenge your thinking, and it will get the job done.
6. Your job as a leader is to teach your people to think strategically. You don't do that by giving them answers. You do it by asking great questions.
7. What seat are you in? Are you in the driver's seat leading change? Are you in the passenger seat letting others drive? Or have you locked yourself in the trunk with a negative mindset? The truth is, we sit in all of them at different times. The opportunity is to be aware which seat you are in and get in the driver's seat as fast as possible.

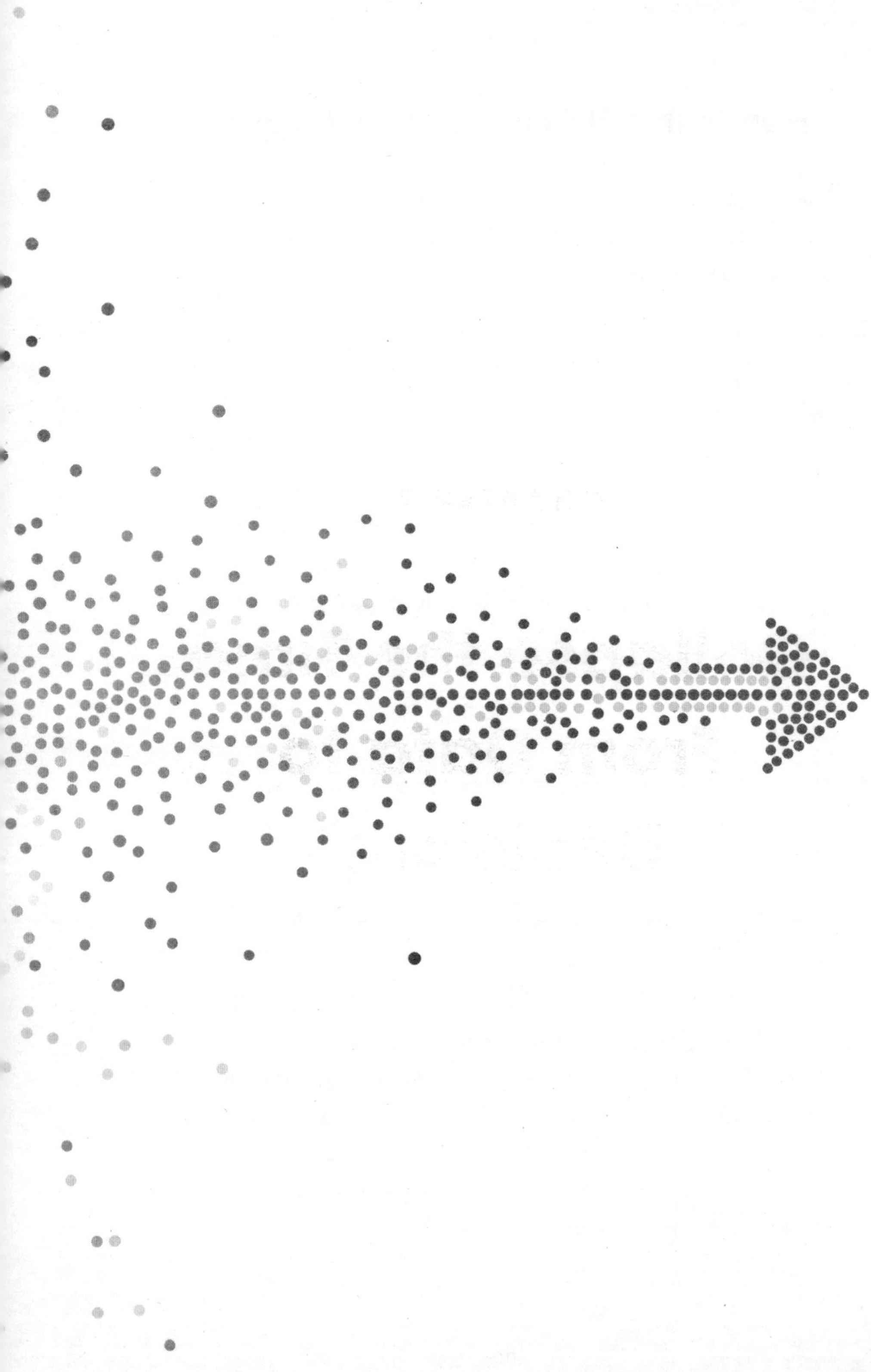

CHAPTER 7

Collapse the Time From Data to Decisions

Turning data into decisions is no easy feat. Today's leaders are often faced with one of two challenges: either they're drowning in too much information, making it difficult to extract meaningful insights, or they don't have access to enough data to make informed decisions. In both cases, the default is to rely on the information in front of them, which can be limited in scope and lead to less-than-optimal decisions. This is where AI comes in as a valuable Thought Partner.

Tim Sharp, a seasoned marketer, recently demonstrated the power of generative AI by creating a fictitious marketing brief for a new Disney theme park in Australia. His process showcased how a company like Disney could leverage AI to create a comprehensive marketing strategy in a matter of minutes.

First, Tim uploaded a CSV file containing de-identified data from 40,000 TripAdvisor reviews of Disney theme parks. He then prompted ChatGPT to analyze customer experiences and provide a high-level summary including key metrics and the top five visitor nationalities in a bar chart.

With the press of a button, the AI quickly analyzed the 40,000 reviews and generated an executive summary. The average rating was an impressive 4.22 out of 5. Reviewers came from 162 unique locations, showcasing Disney's global appeal. It then showed reviews by park, including Disneyland California, Disneyland Paris, and Disneyland Hong Kong.

The AI also created a visual representation of the top five visitor nationalities, including the US, UK, Australia, Canada, and India.

Seeking deeper insights, Tim wanted to conduct a "jobs to be done" analysis. This would uncover the key reasons customers choose a product. He asked the AI to analyze positive and negative reviews and format the results in a table.

As I watched AI respond, it hit me. In a matter of minutes, Tim was able to harness AI to analyze over 40,000 customer reviews, identify the top visitor nationalities, and identify the top reasons for positive and negative reviews. This was incredible.

Tim took it to another level by showing how all this could inform the strategy for a new theme park. Over the next ten minutes I watched him upload images of rival theme parks for competitor analysis, generate potential names for the new theme park, and launch a marketing campaign with social media posts and matching imagery. What would normally take a marketing agency months to accomplish Tim achieved in minutes.

Tim's demonstration was a powerful example of how productive you can become when you combine AI's processing power with your Thought Leadership. In this chapter, I will show you how you can do this as well.

The Data Deluge: Why AI Is Essential

The importance of AI in decision-making becomes clear when we consider the staggering growth of data. According to IDC, the total amount of data created, captured, and consumed globally is projected to soar to 175 zettabytes by 2025. To put this into perspective, if you attempted to store 175 zettabytes on standard DVDs, the stack would reach a height of over twenty-three million miles—nearly one hundred times the distance from the Earth to the moon.

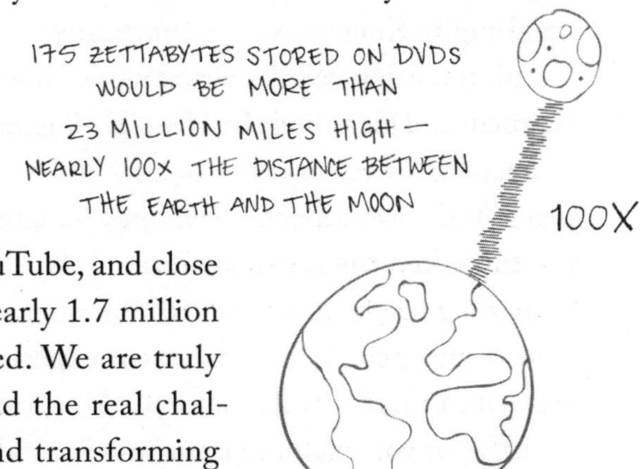

A 2021 Domo report revealed that every minute, 500 hours of video are uploaded to YouTube, and close to 350,000 tweets and nearly 1.7 million Facebook posts are shared. We are truly inundated with data, and the real challenge lies in accessing and transforming this information into actionable insights. Our human abilities simply can't keep up with the pace of data generation, so we often default to whatever's most accessible. This limits our perspective and leads to poor decision-making.

This is where AI changes the game. It takes an average person five hours to read 100,000 tokens. AI collapses that to seconds. The team at Anthropic demonstrated this capability when they uploaded the entire text of The Great Gatsby (72,000 tokens) to their AI, Claude. But there was a catch: they changed one line and asked Claude to find it. Remarkably, Claude scanned the entire novel and pinpointed the change in just twenty-two seconds. That's how fast AI *used to be*. It's even faster now!

OpenAI emphasizes that AI empowers both technical and non-technical teams to analyze information, whether data or images, in a matter of seconds. In the past, you'd have to send data to an analytics team and wait weeks for a response. Now, you can get answers in seconds. You can upload research papers, ask AI to summarize them, and then discuss how to turn that information into actionable insights. Upload CSV files with thousands of entries, and the AI will summarize and extract insights for action. You don't need a data analysis degree to understand data; everyone can do this today.

Sometimes leaders just don't have access to enough quality information. Our businesses are constantly collecting data on customers, but all too often, that information is siloed between departments or trapped in different technology products. So leaders are left scrambling, without an easy way to get their hands on the information they need. And what happens? They end up making decisions based on the limited information that's right in front of them.

Remember: it's tough to read the label when you are inside the box. Your perspective is shaped by your experiences and the information you have at hand. This is limited. As an AI-driven leader, you recognize the importance of getting outside the box and expanding your perspective so you can make the best decisions possible.

That's where AI comes in—it's a powerful tool for accessing data to expand your perspective so you can make smarter decisions. Just ask Frank Iannella, the chief information officer and SVP of digital and technology at Heineken USA. When he heard about generative AI, he decided to learn about it for himself and see how it could help Heineken. What he discovered was eye-opening.

"It was like having a smart assistant with comprehensive knowledge on any subject," Frank explained to me. "I think one of the greatest things about this is, you have this private assistant that can help you brainstorm, come up with fresh ideas, and trigger thoughts you never had before. And it has all of humanity's knowledge, accessible through a natural language interface. It's a total game changer!"

Frank quickly realized that AI is far more than just a content generator. It can actually help you develop ideas and gather information for projects at lightning speed. Seeing AI's immense potential, he decided to put it to the test.

Frank wanted to write a position paper outlining high-level recommendations and guidelines on how Heineken USA's employees could use AI to meet company goals. Normally, this would be a labor-intensive effort requiring extensive research, countless meetings, and content built from scratch. It could easily take months.

But this time, Frank did something different. He asked himself, "How might AI help me do this?"

Frank started by using a tool called Perplexity, an AI platform specializing in research, to find out how companies like Heineken were using AI. He wrote the following prompt:

> Give examples of where CPG companies are using generative AI, split between internal and external customer-facing use cases.

Instantly, Perplexity generated a response highlighting use cases across multiple CPG companies, covering both internal and external customer-facing scenarios. Not yet fully confident in the tool's output, Frank cross-checked the answers to ensure the information was sound.

Viewing this as just the beginning, Frank continued to interact with Perplexity, to generate ideas for how each function within Heineken could leverage AI:

> In a marketing team for a CPG beverage alcohol company, what are the primary ways I could use AI?"

In mere seconds, it generated twenty different use cases.

"That gave me a starting point to go have conversations with the marketing team," Frank told me. Instead of Frank having to start from scratch and conjure up potential use cases himself, AI became a springboard, presenting twenty ideas right off the bat. "From the twenty, maybe ten were relevant, but it was a starting point."

Frank also observed that the quality of the prompt significantly impacted the final responses. He shared, "Context is crucial; the more information I provided, the better and more relevant the generated responses were."

After engaging with business stakeholders and industry contacts, Frank turned back to AI to build out the paper, this time using ChatGPT. He described the task at hand, the desired structure, sample use cases, content collected on how each function was already using the technology, and guidelines for employees on interacting with AI. Working section by section, he collaborated with ChatGPT to whip up some initial drafts, which he then tweaked to fit his writing style and ensure everything flowed smoothly.

Was this perfect right out of the gate? Of course not. Frank understood that AI can get you about 50%–60% of the way on a first draft. But then it's up to you, as the Thought Leader, to review it, add your human touch and judgment, and bring it home. And that's exactly what he did, reviewing it with various stakeholders across the company, including his legal partner, who helped with the necessary edits. After a few rounds of peer reviews with colleagues, bam! The paper was done.

When I asked Frank about the impact AI had on this whole process, he didn't hesitate. **"I probably saved at least 30%–40% of the time it would have taken me to write the paper if I did not use AI. It also provided numerous use cases that we wouldn't have considered otherwise."** Not only did this innovative approach save a ton of time, but it also sparked the exact conversations about the technology that Frank was hoping for. The end result? A comprehensive, strategically aligned position paper for Heineken USA.

I experienced something similar myself while launching AI Leadership. I knew I needed to nail down my brand so that the book, the website, my appearance, *everything* had a unified feel. Specifically, I wanted to define our company's values, voice, target audience, brand colors, fonts for the websites, my personal style, and even what my office should look like. Now, the old-school way of doing this would have meant bringing in a branding agency and spending four to eight weeks on this simply because I didn't have that kind of expertise myself. But with my deadlines looming, I knew I had to get it all figured out in a week, tops.

So I found myself thinking, "How might AI help me do this?" Then it hit me. I wrote up this prompt:

> You're a brand designer for bestselling authors. Your task is to create my brand colors and provide hex codes for each. My topic is AI-driven leadership, and I want to be thought of in the same light as Simon Sinek, Jim Collins, and Peter Drucker. My target audience is executives who are innovative and ambitious and who have decision-making authority to implement projects

> and allocate capital, example: founders, CEOs, chief strategy officers, CIOs, and the venture funds that fund them. I also want you to generate the following for my brand specifically: our core values, the brand voice, our target audience, brand colors, fonts, and fashion that I would wear. Please generate three options.

AI instantly generated three different options. I ended up going with option one. But then I thought, "Why stop there?" So I said:

> Now, can you generate what my office should look like?

In seconds, AI whipped up an image of what it thought my office should look like.

And here's the crazy part—it was spot-on. I'm talking Revere Pewter walls, a bookshelf on the back wall painted this deep, dramatic midnight blue, and gorgeous green accents throughout the space. It was like the AI had read my mind because so much of what it suggested, I already had laid out with a designer. Now, I'm no branding expert, but I needed something done, and fast. AI gave me the ability to step outside the box and harness its amazing processing power to get to a starting point in record time.

I shared this exact branding kit with the person who designed the cover of this book, as well as the agency that built my website. Both were blown away by how prepared I was. This was a real lightbulb moment for me. Because the truth is, I have zero marketing expertise when it comes to building a brand kit. But my big realization was, I don't have to. I just need to know how to wave the baton, write a clear prompt, and engage AI as my Thought Partner. Suddenly, I have all this expertise at my fingertips. Then, if I want to engage a branding expert to take it to the next level, I've laid a solid foundation for them to start with.

The more you learn to harness AI, the more you start to realize just how effective you can become. All those traditional roadblocks that used to stand in the way of getting quality information to make great decisions start to crumble. Suddenly, you have the power to make faster, smarter decisions that can propel your business to new heights.

How AI Transforms Research and Discovery

One of the ways to get access to the right information is to conduct research. The old way of doing this is often to engage an outside firm that can do the market research. It's expensive, and it's slow. AI gives you the ability to do this in mere minutes.

When I started researching this book, I wanted to test two ways. One was to actually hire a research assistant to conduct all the research on the past technological disruptions highlighted in chapter 2. I gave her the scope of what I was looking for, and she was able to turn everything around in two weeks for a $500 investment. I simultaneously did the same work leveraging AI. I was able to generate the majority of the relevant information that I needed for chapter 2, including sources and fact-checking, in under one hour for free.

Learning how to harness AI to conduct research and organize information is a valuable skill that will enhance your decision-making.

COLLAPSE THE TIME TO TURN DATA INTO DECISIONS

Now, let me tell you about one of our customers, Tim O'Sullivan who is the CEO of Boundless AI. Tim is an ambitious, innovative leader who's always looking for ways to leverage AI to deliver more value to clients in less time. And boy, did he deliver.

He was engaged by a late-stage clinical biotech company. They were submitting their first new drug application, focused on the discovery, development, and commercialization of targeted cancer treatments. The company wanted to transition from being perceived merely as an R&D firm to being recognized as a commercial organization with a unique product. To achieve this, the company enlisted Tim and his team to develop their corporate narrative. This included everything from their positioning statement, to defining their value proposition, and articulating their mission, vision, and values.

The traditional way of doing this would have meant hiring a branding agency, waiting six months, and probably dropping $250,000.

Someone would have spent a month doing manual research, pulling documentation, and saving it into files and folders. Then, it would have taken another person two to three weeks to analyze all that data and compile it into factual nuggets. They'd have to review 510(k) filings, which are over 100 pages long, and then conduct a SWOT analysis using competitors to understand the strengths, weaknesses, opportunities, and threats. After that, they'd have to do a positioning exercise to place the competition on a graph and select where they wanted to position themselves for a positioning statement. Finally, they'd have to write the value proposition, mission, vision, and corporate narrative, all while continuously reviewing progress with the client. And if the client changed their perspective (which happens more often than not), the team would have to start all over again.

But Tim? He took a different approach. Instead of asking "How might my team do this?" he asked, "How might AI help us do this?"

With AI, Tim was able to scrape the data from the internet and put it into a database, and then, using AI and some clever prompting, he analyzed the data at mind-blowing speed. As he described this to me, he said with a grin, "What would take a traditional firm months to do, I could do in minutes."

AI worked as Tim's Thought Partner, generating all the research, analysis, SWOT breakdown, and copywriting for the mission, vision, values, and corporate narrative. What would have taken a traditional firm six months to complete Tim and his lean team knocked out in just two weeks, thanks to AI.

But here's the thing—Tim didn't just blindly accept the AI-generated insights. He knew AI's role was to be his Thought Partner, while his role was to be the Thought Leader. As AI generated results, he used his team's seasoned expertise and sound human judgment to validate the outputs. This ensured everything they presented was both factual and accurate.

By partnering with AI, Tim was able to supercharge his team's productivity. As a result, they could serve more customers which drove greater growth, all with less effort, in less time, and at a fraction of the cost to their competition. That is a competitive advantage!

As an AI-driven leader, you have the power to turn data into decisions in a fraction of the time. All you have to do is provide AI with the necessary data, and start collaborating with it. Then, sit back and watch where it takes you.

In the next chapter, we will explore how to overcome the constant pressure to do more with less, which often leads to neglecting the priorities that drive long-term growth. You will learn how to harness AI to balance short-term execution with sustained long-term growth.

"The more you learn to harness AI, the more you start to realize just how effective you can become."

Here's the 20% from This Chapter

1. **Data Overload versus Data Scarcity:** You face two main challenges: drowning in too much information or lacking enough data to make informed decisions, often leading to suboptimal choices.
2. **Speed:** Humans take about five hours to read 100,000 tokens. AI processes the same information in seconds. That's the power of AI.
3. **Accessibility:** Previously, data analysis required waiting weeks for results from an analytics team. Now, AI provides answers in seconds.
4. You don't need a data analysis degree to understand data. AI puts insights right at your fingertips.
5. The more you leverage AI, the more effective you become.
6. AI allows you to utilize skills beyond your own, accelerating your momentum and impact, much like how I used AI to create a marketing brief.

CHAPTER 8

Navigate Short-Term Pressures Without Sacrificing Long-Term Growth

We are no strangers to the constant pressure to do more with less. We feel the heat of delivering results on a short-term or quarterly basis while trying to balance the long-term priorities that will drive sustainable growth and a competitive advantage. But sometimes, we sacrifice the key priorities for long-term growth due to the tyranny of the urgent.

As AI-driven leaders, we have the opportunity to strike a better balance between short-term execution and long-term growth. That means creating space to think, anticipate what's next, and ensure our daily actions are building toward long-term success.

The Impact of Short-Term Thinking

Many businesses today face the pressure to do more with less and deliver results yesterday. When more gets piled onto your plate, what often gets cut? The longer-term strategic priorities that set you up for sustainable growth but don't have an immediate payoff. If you give in to that pressure, you break the chain: your short-term actions don't build your long-term competitive advantage.

A McKinsey Global Institute study found that a whopping 63% of executives admit to delaying new projects that would deliver long-term value, all because they're afraid of missing their quarterly earnings targets. When you're under the gun to deliver short-term results, things like R&D, training your people, and other long-term strategic priorities get shoved to the back burner.

When this happens, you are failing so slowly it can feel like you are succeeding. It's like eating junk food. You can get away with it for a while, but one day you look in the mirror and don't recognize yourself. As an AI-driven leader, your opportunity is to spot this trap and strike the right balance between short-term results and long-term growth.

Drive Long-Term Strategy: Keep Your Eyes on the Horizon

In my experience working with executive teams and facilitating their strategic off-sites, if a long-term vision and goals aren't clearly defined, we've got to put that in place before we focus on the annual strategic plan. Without aligning your people on your long-term vision, it would be like boarding a plane from Los Angeles heading east without a specific destination in mind.

As you lead your team in the AI era, it's critical that you clearly define your long-term vision and the competitive advantages you want to build. This acts as your compass for your annual strategic planning.

Imagine you're the CEO of a major retailer. You're under immense pressure to hit your quarterly numbers, but you know that investing in AI-powered supply chain optimization will give you a huge competitive edge in the long run. You could easily cut that budget to boost short-term profits, but you'd be mortgaging your future.

Instead, you could pull up our AI Thought Partner™ and say:

> I need your help balancing short-term results with long-term growth. I want you to review our strategic plan, then interview me to help me identify what will deliver the most long-term value and where we can deliver quick wins that will keep the board happy while we invest in the future.

After a short conversation with AI asking you questions, it would come back with a prioritized list of initiatives, along with a set of short-term optimizations that will boost efficiency and cut costs without sacrificing long-term investments. Armed with this insight, you can confidently make the case to your board that you're striking the right balance.

> **"This is the power of AI in strategic decision-making. It can help you simulate different scenarios, predict long-term outcomes, and find that sweet spot between delivering short-term results and building a long-term competitive advantage."**

But AI is just one part of the equation. Creating a culture that values long-term thinking is critical as well. You have an opportunity to celebrate the teams that are planting the seeds for future growth, not just the ones that are harvesting the crops today. Make sure your incentive structures reward long-term value creation, not just short-term hits.

Aligning Incentives, Accountability, and the Drive for Long-Term Growth

Strategy is about the competitive advantage you build in the long-term through the actions you take in the short term—and that includes looking at incentives. Why? Because people do what they're incentivized to do.

I experienced this firsthand as chief growth officer for Jindal Steel and Power. The Jindal family and I were constantly discussing the organization's future vision. We wanted to ensure our leaders' actions aligned with that vision, so we examined the incentives. The Jindal family identified three priorities to reward:

1. **Results over effort.** It was about the results delivered, not hours worked.
2. **Year-over-year growth in cash score** (EBITDA minus changes in working capital). EBITDA doesn't pay bills; cash does.
3. **Long-term retention of top talent.** We wanted our best leaders to stick around.

I was tasked with developing a new compensation model that would drive this behavior. I did extensive research and collaborated with the family. Eventually, the plan was approved and implemented for all senior executives across operating companies.

The shift in thinking and actions was immediate. People do what their comp plan rewards. Previously, leaders focused on revenue and EBITDA, but EBITDA isn't cash. You can show strong EBITDA without sufficient cash in the bank.

With compensation tied to cash score, leaders looked beyond EBITDA. They paid attention to working capital norms, inventory levels, and the time to collect receivables.

They started focusing on what would drive year-over-year cash score growth, rather than tactical games to hit quarterly numbers. This meant approving expansion projects that temporarily reduced cash score but enabled long-term gains—a core driver of the company's growth.

Finally, accountability. With a long-term plan and aligned compensation, ongoing accountability is key. The best players always want a great coach to help them get to the next level. This is your job. As a leader, you must ensure your people are focused on the most important actions they can take in the short term to fortify your competitive edge in the long term. Additionally, your role is to develop your team's skills, enabling them to make a bigger impact and take on larger opportunities. This not only drives immediate results but also ensures you have a deep bench for succession planning. The moral of the story? Don't let busyness get in the way of what will grow your business.

The Characteristics of a Strategic Mindset: Seeing the Forest and the Trees

For an AI-driven leader, developing a strategic mindset is essential for driving sustainable growth. But what exactly does that entail? Here are five key characteristics that define a truly strategic mindset:

1. Focus on Your Customers: It's All about Them

Building a long-term competitive advantage requires understanding and uniquely delivering what customers want. As my friend Chris Winton said, "Geoff, right now every leader is asking, 'How do we use AI?' They are asking the wrong question! They should be asking, 'What do our customers want? What are the tools we have that could help us give our customers what they want?' AI is one of those tools." Prioritizing customer needs keeps your strategy relevant and impactful.

2. Turn Vision into Results: The Four Drivers of Growth

It's easy to get caught up in day-to-day firefighting and short-term concerns. Driving growth requires four things: strategy, execution, people, and technology.

- **Strategy:** Cast a vision for what your business will look like in the future with a defensible competitive advantage. Ask, "What is the long-term competitive advantage we want to build? What might results look like? What kind of organization can we become to achieve those things? What might our org chart have to look like to support this vision?"

- **Execution:** Create your strategic plan, outlining the necessary steps you will take this year and who you have to become along the way. Here's what I mean by that. Most companies create their strategic plan around their current team, current resources, and current constraints. That's great if you want to stay where you are but not if you want to level up. Goals should inform who you can become. What talent, resources, or technology might you need to get there? Clarify this, and then take action.
- **People.** The purpose of your people is to achieve your goals. Align your people with your strategic plan. If the plan changes, so should job descriptions. How do your people need to act and grow to get you where you want to go?
- **Technology:** Harness technology to help your people achieve your goals. What technology can free your people up even more to deliver higher value toward your goals? How might technology make your operations more efficient so you get more done with the same resources? How might you weave it into your products or services to reinforce your protective moat?

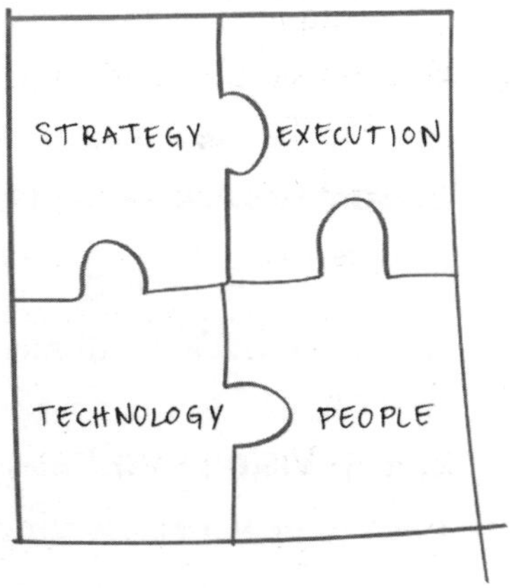

By focusing on the four drivers—strategy, execution, people, technology—you can drive disruptive growth without disrupting your organization.

*If you want to align your strategy, execution, people, and technology—and turn it into results in a fraction of the time—visit AILeadership.com.

3. Cut through the Noise: Prioritize and Communicate:

Effective prioritization is crucial for driving short- and long-term results. When your team is overwhelmed, focusing on 20% priorities that drive 80% of results is vital. This requires strong communication. Prioritization without communication turns strategy into empty plans. Clear communication empowers your team to align their focus, prioritize their work, and deliver the highest returns. It also ensures they don't become reactive or get stuck in the operational weeds.

4. Think Critically, and Act on Data: Enhancing Your Analytical Skills

As you and your team execute your strategic plan, the ability to think critically enables you to navigate the challenges along the way. By analyzing data, you can make decisions based on fact over intuition alone. This combination helps you make informed adjustments to stay on track with your goals.

5. Be Adaptable and Embrace Change

No matter how well you plan, things never go according to plan. AI-driven leaders embrace this and adapt to reality. They understand that change is a constant in business. Instead of resisting it, they view it as an opportunity to gain a competitive advantage. They're open to new ideas, willing to pivot when necessary, and able to navigate moments of uncertainty. This means constantly monitoring the environment, anticipating what could go wrong, and being ready to adjust on the fly.

Adaptability goes further than responding to change. It means proactively seeking it out. Strategic leaders are always looking for ways to innovate, to disrupt their own industries before someone else does.

Here's a great question I learned from Gary Keller:

**"What's the business that will put us out of business?
How can we build it first?"**

Embracing change allows you to stay ahead and turn disruptions into strategic advantages.

This is where AI can be a powerful ally. Not only can it simulate different scenarios to help you make better decisions, but it can be your Thought Partner when change occurs and you're not confident what to do. Just explain the situation to AI and ask it to interview you to help clarify your thinking.

Being an AI-driven leader means having the skill to ask the right questions and leveraging data and technology to search for the right answers. This keeps you in the driver's seat as Thought Leader and AI as your Thought Partner. By cultivating these five characteristics, you can develop a truly strategic mindset that will serve you well today and into the future. It's not easy, but the payoff of building sustainable competitive advantages and driving lasting success for your organization, is immense.

Get Started with Your Strategic Thinking

How do you get started? Start by blocking time for some strategic thinking.

Here are some questions for you to consider:

1. What long-term competitive advantage are you building?
2. How do you know if it's defensible and will lead to success?
3. What would your business need to look like to realize this advantage?

4. Based on that, what must you achieve this year to make meaningful progress toward your long-term vision?
5. Where do you need to recommit time and resources for maximum impact?
6. What are you currently saying yes to that's distracting you from what matters most?
7. What can you do about it?

I find immense value in strategic thinking sessions where I put pen to paper and wrestle with questions like these. As I've mentioned, AI is meant to enhance your thinking, not replace it. While I leverage AI daily, I still rely on an old-fashioned pen and paper for strategic thinking. It's a muscle I want to keep strong. Once I've done my initial reflection, I turn to my AI Thought Partner™ to see how it can expand my perspective.

You can do the same. I've trained our AI Thought Partner™ on the questions above. I encourage you to do this with our AI Thought Partner™, as it has been trained for this kind of conversation, where other AI models have not. Here's the prompt:

> I want you to act as a strategic Thought Partner in helping me reevaluate if our short-term actions are aligned with our long-term vision. Please interview me to help think this through, and give me feedback on where my thinking is solid and where you see areas for improvement.

To put this into action, scan this QR code or visit AiLeadership.com.

Remember, AI-driven leadership is about continuously aligning your people and technology to deliver on both short-term and long-term results. As the composer of strategy, your role is to see the big picture and understand how the pieces fit together. As the conductor of teams and technology, ensure your people and tech are always in harmony. Here are some practical ways you can put this chapter into action.

Harness AI to Support Long-Term Strategic Thinking

AI can be a powerful ally in long-term strategic thinking. Here's how:

SCENARIO PLANNING AND SIMULATIONS

Scenario planning and simulations are invaluable for visualizing the potential impact of your decisions, helping you avoid pitfalls and uncover blind spots. With AI as your Thought Partner, you can process vast amounts of data to simulate future scenarios and anticipate how customers might react. This helps you make better decisions to achieve your goals.

Try this prompt:

> I want you to act as our ideal customer, (describe your customer), in reviewing the attached proposal. Simulate how they might respond by providing me with feedback on:
>
> 1. What you like about our proposal.
> 2. What you do not like about it or things that may not make sense to you.
> 3. The top changes we can make to ensure this proposal is something you would agree to.

THE EXECUTIVE COACH

An executive coach's value lies in asking great questions that clarify your thinking, prioritize your actions, and expose your blind spots. We've all been stuck in the operational weeds, losing sight of the big picture. A great coach can be invaluable in these moments. While AI can't replace a human coach, it can certainly enhance the coaching experience.

Here's how to engage AI as a coaching companion. Share your long-term goals, and have AI act as an executive coach, asking questions to evaluate if you're focusing on the right things today to achieve your long-term vision.

> I am an executive looking to ensure that what I am focusing on in the short term not only helps us achieve our goals this year but is also in alignment with our long-term goals. Act as my executive coach and ask me one question at a time to:
>
> 1. Understand our long-term goals.
> 2. Understand what I am prioritizing in the short term.
> 3. Evaluate if I am focusing on the right things in the short term to achieve our long-term goals.
>
> Please help me identify any potential blind spots and prioritize my actions to stay on track.

THE BOARD MEMBER

The board's role includes hiring/firing the CEO, approving strategy, identifying risks, and representing stakeholders's long-term interests. They're inherently focused on the long game. Simulating a board member with AI can be incredibly valuable.

Greg Shove, CEO of Section, an education tech company that we are strategic partners with, did exactly this. He used AI to prepare for a board meeting, uploading his deck and asking AI to role-play an aggressive, growth-minded board member and highlight potential questions. AI generated a solid list of questions, which Greg used to prepare.

During the actual meeting, Greg's team compared the board's questions to AI's. Remarkably, AI predicted the real board's questions with 91% accuracy. Greg realized AI could greatly enhance board meeting prep and encouraged his board to leverage AI for even more value in future meetings.

You don't need a real board to use AI this way. Having board-level thinking at your fingertips can help align short-term execution with long-term vision and expose blind spots.

Engaging your AI board lets you consider various futures, enhance your thinking, and increase your company's odds of weathering any storm.

Try this prompt:

> I want you to act as a growth-minded board member and review our strategic plan. What questions or potential concerns do you have based on our deck? Put a focus on ensuring we are striking the right balance between short-term execution and long-term growth.

EMPOWER YOUR TEAMS TO THINK STRATEGICALLY

Your job as a leader is to deliver results by teaching your people to think strategically. They need to understand the long-term competitive advantage you are working to build so they can prioritize their actions to drive progress.

When advising executives to empower strategic thinking in their teams, I suggest these steps:

1. Ask your team to articulate your long-term strategy. If they can't, that's okay. It just means you have an opportunity to help elevate their strategic thinking.
2. Ask them what key priorities they should focus on now. How do these priorities align with short-term goals and long-term strategy? Do you agree with their thinking, or do you need to help them align with what you see as the leader?
3. Are there things they feel they can be prioritizing for the long-term strategy that aren't getting enough attention due to short-term pressures?
4. What do they think they can do to strike the correct balance between short-term execution and long-term growth?

These questions are all about strategy. You don't need AI to ask them. Without clarity on your questions as the Thought Leader, AI can become a shiny distraction. But once you've organized your thoughts, consider if AI can support you.

These are just a few examples of how AI can accelerate your strategic momentum. By embedding AI into your decision-making processes, you can move faster and with greater precision. You can spend less time bogged down in data analysis and more time focused on high-level strategy and vision.

But it's not just about speed. It's also about the quality of your decisions. With AI as your Thought Partner, you can consider a wider range of options, challenge your assumptions, and uncover hidden opportunities. You can make decisions that are not only fast but also deeply informed and strategically sound.

In the next chapter, I will show you how.

Here's the 20% from This Chapter

1. The pressure to deliver immediate results often leads to sacrificing long-term growth priorities. Giving in to this pressure breaks the chain between your actions today and your competitive advantage tomorrow.
2. Strike the right balance between achieving short-term results and building long-term competitive advantages for sustainable growth.
3. Focus on the four key drivers of growth:
   - **Strategy:** Build a long-term competitive advantage through short-term actions.
   - **Execution:** Use your strategic plan as a compass to guide your actions.
   - **People:** Align your team with the strategic plan, focusing on the 20% that drives 80% of the results.
   - **Technology:** Leverage technology to enhance efficiency and free up your team.
4. Constantly align your people and technology to achieve both short-term and long-term goals. As the composer of strategy, see the big picture and understand how all the pieces fit together. As the conductor, ensure your people and technology work in harmony.

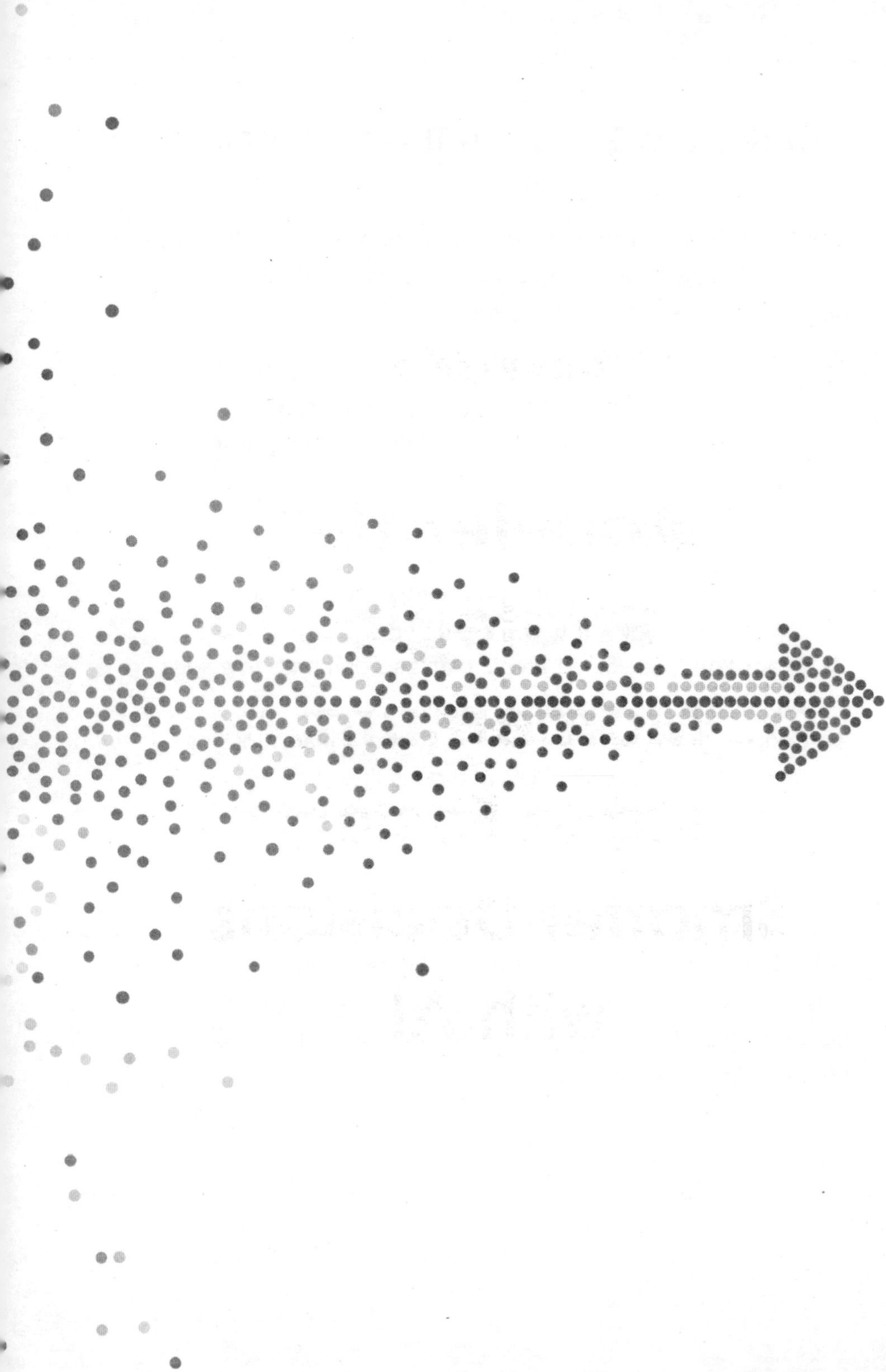

CHAPTER 9

Accelerate Strategic Momentum: Make Faster, Smarter Decisions with AI

Grady Davis is a top-tier executive in the medical device space that I've advised. He's a visionary, constantly pushing his team to get better. One day, Grady and I found ourselves deep in conversation about artificial intelligence. His eyes lit up with excitement. He had dabbled with AI, using it to generate marketing content. But strategic decision-making? That was a whole new ballgame for him. I asked him what his biggest challenge was.

He explained that when a patient has a medical device implanted, maintaining communication and follow-up becomes extremely difficult for both the physician and the medical device company. This is especially true for patients who had the procedure as children but were now adults. Over their lives, they moved, and their names could have changed. His team was tasked with tackling this issue. It wasn't just about finding a needle in a haystack; it was about finding a needle in a constantly shifting haystack.

I asked Grady what he had done so far. He explained he had put together a team of five, dedicating their full-time efforts to this Herculean task. For two months, they had been focusing on this problem, and they had finally come up with some potential strategies.

I leaned in. "Great. Watch this." I shared my screen, revealing the AI interface. I wrote a detailed prompt and hit enter.

The AI didn't miss a beat. It spat out five answers. Instantly. Grady's eyes widened as he read the responses. "Geoff," he said, "these are really good answers. I want to compare these with what my team came up with."

Weeks later, Grady and I reconvened. He was noticeably excited. **"Geoff, this is incredible. What you showed me could collapse hundreds of hours of work into minutes!"**

Grady's story represents a pivotal moment you will experience as you become an AI-driven leader: recognizing AI's potential to transform your decision-making. His team invested hundreds of hours into a tough problem. Despite the significant barriers they faced, they generated great solutions. But what could his team achieve if they weren't hamstrung by all their current obstacles and could harness AI's processing power in everything they did? Grady realized this could put his team in a completely different league.

Here's why this matters to you. The decisions you make can either grow your business or put you out of business. With AI as your Thought Partner, you can streamline your process and make faster, smarter decisions. Instead of doing all the work at each step of the decision-making process, you can engage AI to supercharge your knowledge and judgment with its processing power. This unlocks the value of your people.

In this chapter, I will walk you through the seven steps of the decision-making process. You'll see how AI can serve as your Thought Partner at each step, collapsing the time it takes to make great decisions. This allows you to focus on what truly matters: driving the growth of your business and creating opportunities for your people.

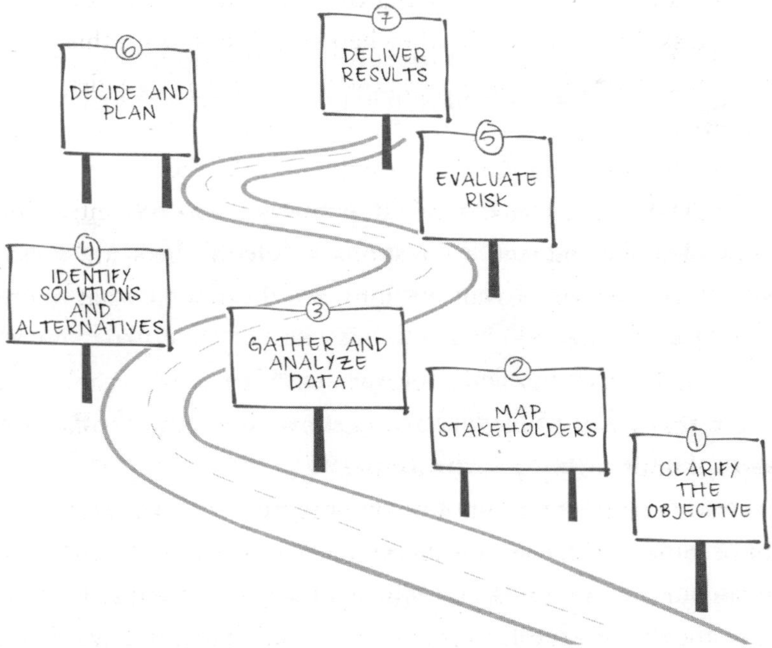

The Strategic Decision-Making Framework

Making great decisions can be broken down into seven key steps:

1. Clarify the Objective
2. Map Stakeholders
3. Gather and Analyze Information
4. Identify Solutions and Alternatives
5. Evaluate Risks
6. Decide and Plan Implementation
7. Deliver Results

Step 1: Clarify the Objective

The first and most crucial step in the decision-making process is to clarify the objective by addressing two key points:

1. You're addressing a real problem, not just a symptom.
2. The problem aligns with your goals and isn't just a shiny distraction.

For leaders, it's easy to mistake symptoms for problems. Think of it like this: tackling smoke doesn't extinguish the fire. You can wave away the smoke all day, but until you put out the flames, you haven't solved the core issue. When defining your objective, make sure you're aiming at the root problem, not just the smoke.

Next, check if your objective aligns with your goals. Remember, saying yes to one thing means saying no to something else. With your limited resources—time, money, and attention—ensure your objective aligns with your goals. If it doesn't, it might be time to refocus and consider whether going through the decision-making process will truly impact your business.

HERE'S HOW AI CAN HELP

AI can serve as your strategic Thought Partner, challenging your assumptions and ensuring that you're tackling the root problem, not just a symptom. It can test for alignment by evaluating how solving this issue fits into your goals and long-term competitive advantage. Additionally, AI can help you weigh the opportunity cost by asking you, "If you focus on this, what will you have to say no to?" Ultimately, you can leverage AI to ensure that your objective is a wise investment of your time and resources.

Step 2: Map Stakeholders

With clarity on your objective, the next step is to identify all the stakeholders required to support this change for it to last. This includes four categories of people:

1. **Decision-Makers:** The people who can approve or reject the decision
2. **Influencers:** The people who can influence the decision-makers in their decisions
3. **Champions:** The people who will champion the change among the stakeholders
4. **Early Adopters:** The people most affected by the decision who can represent the wider group

Often, this step of mapping stakeholders is skipped or only partially executed. Leaders might just make the call themselves or check in with a few other executive stakeholders, usually the ones they need approval from anyway. But the influencers, the ones who can really sway decision-makers' opinions, are often overlooked. That's a recipe for decisions getting stuck later on.

The greatest missed opportunity lies in not involving the early adopters, the very people who are going to be directly impacted by the decision. Some of your greatest insights are going to come from the people who are closest to where the rubber meets the road. If the goal is to make the best decision possible, then you would be crazy not to make sure this group has a voice in the process.

“

Some of your greatest insights are going to come from the people who are closest to where the rubber meets the road. If the goal is to make the best decision possible, then you would be crazy not to make sure this group has a voice in the process.

”

When you make a decision from the top down without looping these people in, you're not just limiting your own perspective; you're setting yourself up for a major "people problem" down the line. And trust me on this: when people feel like they've been left out, it breeds resentment and resistance that can seriously derail your progress. But when you bring them in early, you tap into a wealth of valuable insights and create a sense of ownership that can make things run a whole lot smoother.

HERE'S HOW AI CAN HELP

AI can enhance your thinking in this step so you have deeper context in a fraction of the time. Here's a prompt I used when making a decision at Jindal Steel & Power:

I need to make a decision for our business and want to be strategic about involving the right people in the process. Acting as my Thought Partner, I want you to interview me by asking one question at a time to help me answer the following questions:

1. Who are the decision-makers who can approve or reject this decision?
2. Who are the influencers who can sway the thinking of the decision-makers I need to engage?
3. Who are early adopters who will be most affected by the decision because they are closest to the point of impact?

Then, help me analyze what each person cares about and how the decision impacts them. This will help me communicate the benefits and mitigate potential downsides.

Structure your answer in a table format.

Our AI Thought Partner™ is trained on this prompt. The next time you need to map your stakeholders, just ask it to help you.

With AI as your Thought Partner, you can quickly identify the key decision-makers, influencers, and early adopters. But it doesn't stop there. You can ask AI to adopt the persona of one of these people to simulate how they might respond to the situation. This way, you can anticipate objections and refine your approach.

Want to take it a step further? Have AI role-play with you as that person so you can practice the conversation, and then have AI give you feedback on how to improve your approach.

Role-play with me as if you are the decision maker. I'll present a recommendation for your approval, and I want you to simulate their likely response. Challenge me where they might resist so

I can practice my responses. Afterward, provide feedback on:

1. What I did well.
2. Where my approach was not strong enough.
3. The key changes I can make to increase my odds of success.

Here's why this matters: **the success of your communication is determined by the way it is received, not your intention.** If your stakeholders can't understand the value you intend to deliver, then you will fail.

Roleplaying with AI is something I do regularly to ensure my communication hits the mark. Every time I do this, I get at least one valuable insight that can boost my influence as a leader. Try this approach to elevate your communication, and watch your impact soar.

Step 3: Gather and Analyze Information

Making a great decision requires having access to the right information. The problem is, gathering and analyzing all the necessary information is not easy. Traditionally, companies collect data across different departments—sales, marketing, operations—but each piece is kept in its own little silo. To get a comprehensive view, you have to manually request and combine reports from each department. This process is time-consuming and inefficient, especially when you don't have a simple way to see what data even exists in your company.

Getting access to all that information means you have to rely on multiple people with competing priorities to stop what they're doing and get you what you need. If one department drags its feet, it slows you down. Then, you have to organize and review it, which takes more time. And that's if your business has the data! What if your business doesn't? Then you're stuck making decisions based on gut feelings or incomplete information or shelling out for expensive market research reports.

HERE'S HOW AI CAN HELP

With the right data strategy, AI can take all that scattered data and turn it into valuable insights in minutes, not weeks. While centralizing data is a long-term goal, AI helps you overcome current inefficiencies. Even if your data access is limited, AI tools can quickly answer specific questions and sometimes even provide source validation.

For companies without a solid data strategy, AI tools offer quick research and idea validation. And if you've got centralized data, AI-driven tools let you interact with your data in real time and get instant answers. Bottom line, with AI, you can have access to higher-quality information in a fraction of the time.

Step 4: Identify Solutions and Alternatives

You've clarified your objective, mapped your stakeholders, and gathered valuable insights from your data. Now it's time to start generating solutions. There are many ways you can approach this. Sometimes you sit down for some solo thinking time. Maybe you rally your team to brainstorm. Or you might engage industry experts and advisors. Regardless what approach you take, remember what we learned in chapter 6: you have biases and assumptions that, when left unchallenged, can lead you astray. You've got to challenge them head-on.

The key is to search beyond the initial list of obvious ideas and push for non-obvious alternatives. It's easy to mistake *a* solution for *the* solution, but by considering all the possibilities, you can make better-informed decisions with the best ideas front and center.

HERE'S HOW AI CAN HELP

AI can be a valuable Thought Partner by generating ideas and uncovering non-obvious alternatives. With AI, you're not limited to the mental horsepower of yourself and your team. As the Thought Leader, you can focus AI's processing power to generate additional ideas in seconds. Then, you get to apply your judgment to the enhanced list, zeroing in on the best options.

Step 5: Evaluate Risks

Your ability to think strategically and make great decisions is the difference between growing your business and going out of business. What's the secret sauce? Evaluating risk! Now that you have solutions, it's time to consider how you might be wrong and what the fallout could be if things don't go according to plan. As an optimist, I'm all about focusing on the upside of a solution. But sometimes, I forget to consider the potential downsides. It took some learning for me to start asking, "What's the downside? Am I willing to live with the downside?"

To make a great decision, you have to pressure test your solutions. Traditionally we rally our teams to ask "How might this go wrong?" It's a solid starting point, but remember, our perspective is limited. It's tough to read the label when you are inside the box.

HERE'S HOW AI CAN HELP

Here's a prompt you can use to get you outside the box when it comes to evaluating risk:.

> I need to make an important decision. Here is the situation: (describe the situation). Here are the solutions I have identified so far: (list the solutions you've identified). I want you to act as

> an expert in identifying risk by asking me one question at a time to help me see the second-order consequences of these solutions.

AI quickly leverages its processing power to identify potential risks you might have missed. It's like having an extra set of eyes that can see what you might miss. From there, you can apply your judgment to evaluate if the risks are valid and what you can do to mitigate them.

Step 6: Decide and Plan

It's time to make your decision and plan how to make it happen. Traditionally, decision-makers might rely on their gut instincts or past experiences, or they may simply pull rank. Or they might get caught up in endless meetings with senior leaders, going back and forth on different options. Once a decision is finally made, the manual planning process kicks in—involving a whole lot of coordinating across teams and departments, scheduling meetings, and putting together the plan using tools like spreadsheets and project management software.

More often than not, key stakeholders and external consultants get involved, but the process might not do a great job of challenging biases or assumptions. This can lead to plans that aren't quite hitting the mark. The effectiveness of the plan is only as good as the knowledge and experience of those involved, and any blind spots or gaps in understanding can hold it back.

HERE'S HOW AI CAN HELP

On top of your traditional approach, bring in AI as your Thought Partner. Try something like this:

> I need to make an important decision. I'm considering these two options. Your task is to evaluate the upside and downside of each potential solution and explain which you'd recommend and why.

In no time at all, AI will give you a recommendation, and as the Thought Leader, you get to make the final call.

When it comes to planning the implementation, AI can dramatically cut down the time it takes to draft your plan. If you don't have a model for an implementation plan, just ask AI to generate one. It should get you about 50%–60% of the way there. Then, as the Thought Leader in the driver's seat, you can apply your judgment and context to fine-tune it into a workable model.

Once you have your model, have AI fill out the plan and make sure all the necessary details are included. If you need more information, just ask! If you already have a model, AI can fill it out based on the template you give it. Plus, AI can review and strengthen the plan by spotting weaknesses and suggesting improvements, even adopting different personas to really put the plan through its paces.

Step 7: Deliver Results

As a leader, your job is to deliver results. Period. Even once you've made a decision and put it into action, you're not done yet! There's a big difference between making the decision right and making the right decision. If you have followed this decision-making framework so far, then you've made the decision right. That means your decision is a hypothesis. To know if you've made the right decision, you need to deliver results. That's where the three-step process comes in: implement, evaluate, and iterate.

We are shifting away from an industrial mindset and toward an AI-driven mindset. It's a move from "learn a skill once; apply forever" to "learn constantly; thrive continuously." When it comes to our decisions, it's a shift from "make the right decision" to "make the decision and then implement, evaluate, and iterate to deliver the result." This can be a challenge for some leaders. In my advisory experience, I've come across leaders who tied their sense of success to the decisions they made rather than the results they delivered. It was pretty clear when the decision they made didn't pan out, and they were unwilling to acknowledge it because they were afraid of looking bad. They cared more about appearances than results. They made themselves the immovable object, which meant the goal had to move.

As an AI-driven leader, you are navigating uncharted territory when it comes to adopting AI in your organization. Not every decision you make is going to deliver the expected results. What matters is making the decision right and then having the humility to admit that you could still be wrong. If you commit to implementing the decision, then evaluating the performance, and iterating when the plan isn't going according to plan, then you boost your chances of delivering the result.

HERE'S HOW AI CAN HELP

Think of AI as your continuous improvement partner. It can crunch the numbers to see how things are tracking against your goals. When you are falling behind and struggling to identify strategies to bridge the gap, turn to AI. For too long we've relied on our own knowledge to figure out how to achieve our goals. By combining AI's processing power with your own judgment, you create a powerful strategic synergy.

The key to remember is AI is not a substitute for your judgment and experience as a leader. While AI can rapidly process data and give you options, the final decision is yours. You are the Thought Leader. AI is your Thought Partner.

As we conclude Part 2 on becoming an AI-driven leader, you've envisioned what the future of your leadership might look like in an AI-driven world and how you can start harnessing AI to make faster, smarter decisions. In Part 3, we'll shift our focus to building an AI-driven organization. We'll explore practical steps, from leading with strategic clarity year-round, to executing your strategic plans, to laying out a roadmap for seamless AI adoption, and increasing the impact of every employee by 10x. This is where the rubber meets the road and theory turns into action so you can drive growth.

> **"By combining AI with your own judgment, you create a powerful strategic synergy."**

Here's the 20% from This Chapter

To make faster, smarter decisions, follow the strategic decision-making framework:

1. **Clarify the Objective:** Make sure you are solving the problem, not a symptom.
2. **Map Stakeholders:** Determine your decision-makers, influencers, champions, and early adopters.
3. **Gather and Analyze Information:** Get the best information to inform the best decisions.
4. **Identify Solutions and Alternatives:** Push beyond the initial list. The best idea wins.
5. **Evaluate Risks:** How might this go wrong? Are you willing to live with the downside?
6. **Decide and Plan Implementation.**
7. **Deliver Results:** Implement your plan. Evaluate your results, and iterate until you deliver what was committed.

Part Three

Build an AI-Driven Organization

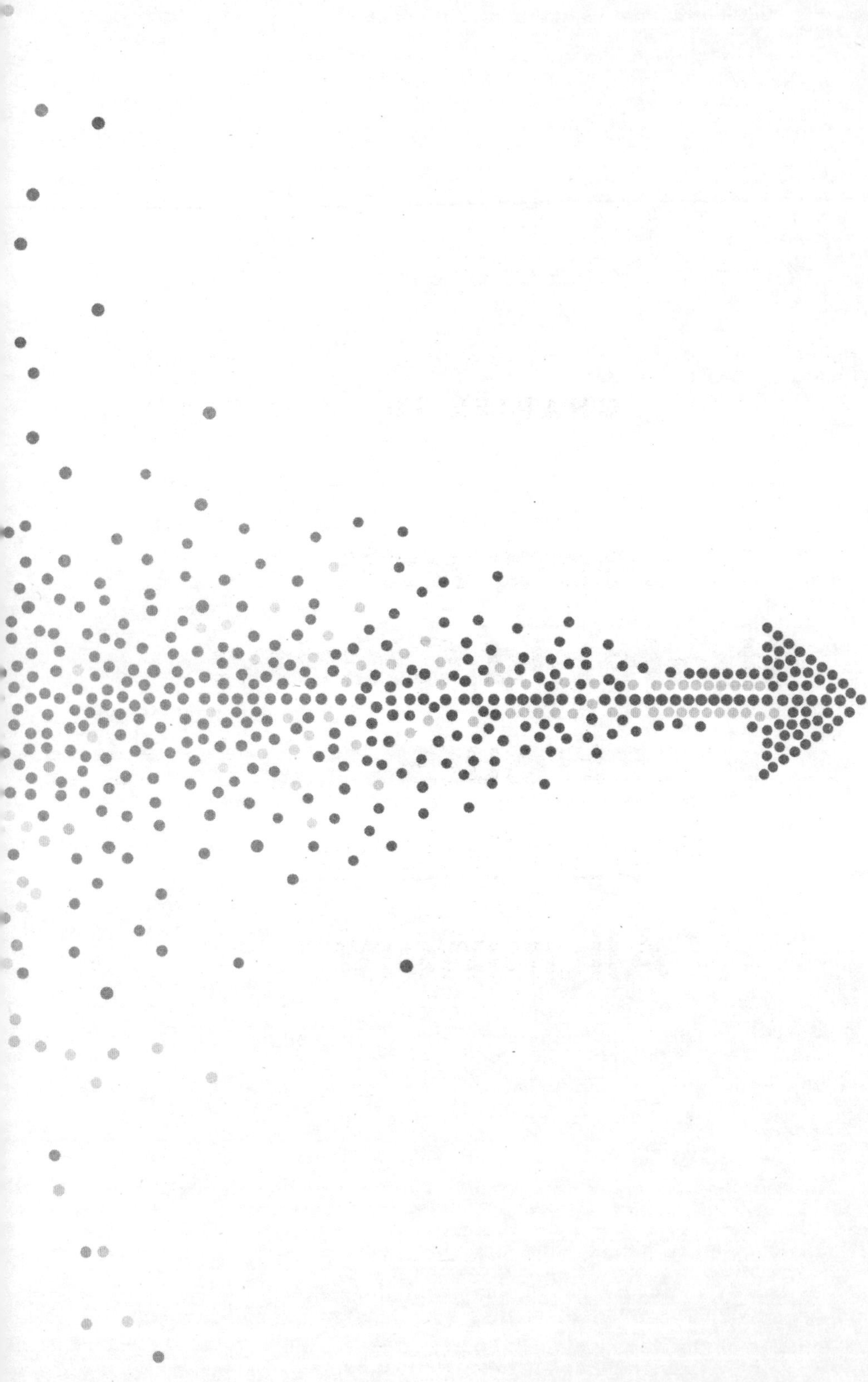

CHAPTER 10

Lead with Strategic Clarity: Ensure Year-Round Alignment

Herbalife is a forty-plus-year-old global brand with operations in over ninety countries. They're in the middle of a massive transformation to become the world's premier health and wellness platform. The stakes could not be higher.

Enter Stephan Gratziani, the CEO. Stephan and his leadership team had defined what they called their six bold moves. These were the strategic bets that would drive the company's future. The challenge was creating real alignment across the C-suite and market directors from every region around the world.

Now, the old way to do this? You'd have a traditional off-site with sticky notes and Sharpies. A facilitator would guide the conversation with one person talking at a time. In this setting, the loudest voices dominate, the smartest ideas may go unsaid, and politics hold people back from saying what they really feel. It feels like alignment, but it's not. People simply nod their heads because it feels safe, not because they genuinely buy in. The whole process feels like it takes forever, stretching across a series of meetings over three to six months.

This approach is officially over.

As their AI strategy execution partner, we were brought in to do this the AI-driven way. Instead of sticky notes and Sharpies with one person talking at a time, we architected a series of prompts in our AI Thought Partner™.

We gathered the entire executive team plus the market directors from around the world at Herbalife's headquarters in Los Angeles. Everyone clicked a button, and the AI Thought Partner™ simultaneously interviewed each person in the room in a secure environment. It asked them what they liked about the bold moves; what they didn't understand; what they saw as risks to execution on a global level versus a regional level; what barriers the executive team would have to clear for them to be successful; and how the culture would have to shift as they navigated this transformation. AI interviewed them for about twenty minutes and generated a detailed report of every person's thinking.

Then, we clicked another button. AI simultaneously read the reports and synthesized everything into one shared view. On the screen, it displayed where people were aligned and where they were not. Based on that, it posed various questions to the room. AI stepped into the role of co-facilitator alongside me. It listened to everything being discussed in real time, compressed the conversation, and asked the next best question to drive the group toward deeper alignment. This process repeated for two hours.

What would have normally taken three to six months of meetings was done in a matter of hours.

The impact was so significant that the executive team said, "How can we expand this?" They brought us to Vienna for their annual conference. First, we met with four hundred distributors and facilitated a similar exercise. These were the people who would lead the change on the ground. The old way to earn their buy-in would have been months of listening campaigns and one-on-one conversations. We collapsed that into a two-hour AI-driven session. Then, we expanded it further and architected a prompt that, in just twenty minutes, unlocked the voices of four thousand distributors.

If you want change to last, you have to win the hearts and minds of your people. This means their voices must be heard, because authorship creates ownership.

This isn't just a faster way to align. It is a fundamentally different way to run the business.

The Million-Dollar Question: Are You Truly Committed To Strategic Thinking?

The Herbalife story illustrates something bigger than one company's transformation. It reveals a fundamental truth: **most companies were**

not designed to move at the speed AI requires.

Strategic clarity cannot stay trapped in the head of the CEO or live on a static document. The world is moving too fast, so clarity has to be shared and become alive. The companies that win in the AI era will be the ones that can turn strategy into results the fastest.

Three common problems often undermine your ability to lead with the highest level of strategic clarity needed to drive growth:

1. **Not Thinking Big Enough:** Leaders often limit their goals to what they believe is achievable with their current resources and capabilities. This conservative approach anchors you to the way things used to be instead of freeing you to imagine who you can become and what you can achieve.
2. **Lack of Clarity and Alignment:** Most leadership teams are not truly aligned. They may sit in the same room, nod, and repeat the strategy, but that is not the same as deep clarity and real buy-in. You cannot march a team toward winning in the market if they don't clearly understand what winning looks like and believe in the path to get there.
3. **Lack of an AI-Driven Strategy Execution System:** Even when organizations create alignment, most don't have a structure to sustain it, update it, and translate it into results as reality changes. They create plans, but not a living system that keeps strategy, priorities, people, and action moving together.

In this chapter, I'll show you how to overcome these common pitfalls and lead with strategic clarity throughout the year. I'll also show you how AI is fundamentally changing the way leaders create alignment and drive execution.

Problem 1: Not Thinking Big Enough Solution: Expand Who You Can Become

I've seen it time and time again: executive teams playing small with their goals. They set targets based on what they think they can achieve, believing their plan is sufficient if all the elements add up to the goal. But here's the problem: they're capping their potential and leaving money on the table.

The true purpose of a goal is to act as a compass, guiding you toward who you can become. Don't base your goals on what you think you can do. Instead, think big and launch yourself onto a completely new trajectory.

I saw this play out with a power company I advised. The CEO had received a mandate from the board to increase free cash flow from $525 million to $725 million in the next fiscal year. The board sweetened the pot with an incentive to the executive team: hit $850 million in free cash flow, and there would be a big payout.

The board brought me in to advise and guide the executive team to drive this growth. When we gathered the leadership team, the air was thick with doubt and skepticism. Go from $525 million to $725 million in free cash flow in just twelve months? That alone seemed crazy—but $850 million? It was so big that some leaders wondered if it was even worth trying.

"The true purpose of a goal is to act as a compass, guiding you toward who you can become. Don't base your goals on what you think you can do. Instead, think big and launch yourself onto a completely new trajectory."

I looked around the room and asked, "How many of you know exactly what you are capable of achieving?" Crickets.

I laid it out for them: the truth is, none of us really know what our true potential is. But when we're setting goals, if we can't see a straight shot to achieving them, we convince ourselves it can't be done. That's a story we are telling ourselves, not a fact. We don't know it to be true.

We talked about how the purpose of a goal is to inform who we can become. That means we needed to suspend our disbelief and imagine what a plan to hit $850 million *might* look like. From there, we can ask ourselves, "Who can we become to turn this plan into results? How might we structure our teams and leverage technology to help us get there?" The leaders rolled up their sleeves and got to work.

Over the next several hours, the executive team knocked it out of the park! They thought outside the box to pinpoint the most important priorities that would drive the biggest impact in the business. I remember when one leader had a huge grin on his face and said, "We did it!" I asked him what he meant. "I just ran the numbers. If we achieve everything in this plan, we'll hit $850 million in free cash flow!"

I took a moment to gauge the reactions around the room. Heads were nodding, and there was a clear sense of satisfaction on everyone's face. A number that had seemed impossible at the start of the day suddenly felt within reach. I turned back to the leader and asked, "Let me ask you this: how often do plans go according to plan?"

He didn't miss a beat. "Never."

I nodded in agreement. I praised the team for their incredible work so far, but I didn't mince words: "You don't have a plan to succeed. You have a plan to fail!" The room went so quiet you could have heard a pin drop.

This is the first problem leaders face: not thinking big enough. When they create a plan, if everything in the plan adds up to the goal, they think they've got a winner. But every plan looks great until it collides with reality. If everything in this plan has to go off without a hitch for them to hit $850 million, and we know that's not going to happen, then we know we have a plan to fail.

I explained that depending on the type of company, we should have a buffer above and beyond the plan. I turned to the CEO and asked him how much he thought we'd need to feel confident. He didn't hesitate: "$1 billion in free cash flow." The room went quiet. They had stretched themselves to the max to get to $850 million. How in the world could they get to $1 billion?

This is when I reminded them that the purpose of a goal is not to achieve a result but to inform who we can become as leaders to achieve that goal. I fired off some questions:

1. What would have to be true over the next year for $1 billion in free cash flow to be possible?
2. What resources would we need to secure that we don't currently have?
3. What would our team need to look like?
4. Where would we have to harness technology?
5. What are we currently saying yes to that we'd have to say no to so we could free ourselves up to focus on higher-level strategies?

The executives got back to work, challenging their assumptions and pushing the boundaries of their thinking. By the time we wrapped up the off-site, all the elements of their plan added up to $1 billion in free cash flow.

None of us truly know our full potential. As AI-driven leaders, we must challenge our conventional thinking to break through the barriers limiting our achievements.

Over the next year, this team ran into plenty of challenges they never saw coming. **But by the end of the year, this team that had been skeptical of growing from $525 million to $725 million? They grew to $828 million in free cash flow!**

Here's the truth: we limit ourselves by setting goals based on what we think is doable. We let our current skills, resources, and comfort zones dictate what's possible. As a result, we don't push our thinking or planning hard enough. Then, when plans inevitably go off the rails and the gap between the goal and reality gets too wide, we throw in the towel. When you set goals based on what you think you can achieve, you are putting a ceiling over your achievement and leaving money on the table.

The problem is, thinking bigger is challenging because most people's minds are not used to being stretched that far. Most people have believed their entire career that the purpose of a goal is to achieve a result. But the moment you stop viewing it as a finish line to cross and start seeing it as a compass to guide who you can become? That's when you realize it's not about hitting the number. It's about expanding who you are and what's possible.

As you review your goals, ask yourself, "Were our goals set based on what we thought we could achieve, or did we set them to push us to grow to the next level? How might we think even bigger?" Set a goal that scares you, and then outline a plan with the specific steps to make that goal a reality. You can still budget around more conservitive metrics, but align your people's actions on a higher trajectory. Worst-case scenario, you fall short. But the real benefit is that you'll challenge yourself to let go of what got you here and embrace what will propel you to the next level.

Problem 2: Lack of Clarity and Alignment Solution: Build Real Alignment, Not the Illusion of It

In 2024, I was brought in to deliver an AI workshop for an executive team at their strategic off-site. I walked into the room and was greeted by a wall covered with large Post-it notes, each detailing the priorities the executive team had been focusing on for the past six months. On each Post-it were smaller hot pink, neon yellow, and orange sticky notes, with even more priorities scribbled across them in black Sharpie.

It was clear that their strategic wheels were turning, but things somehow went sideways. I sat and listened as the leadership team talked about the progress they had made and what they thought they needed to focus on for the rest of the year.

Ten minutes went by where the conversation bounced around like a pinball, from one topic to the next. I found myself extremely confused, wondering, "What is our goal?"

At that moment, they realized that the majority of their focus had been scattered across new product launches that made a small impact on the overall goal. Meanwhile, growing the market share of their flagship product, which would drive the majority of their growth, had been getting zero focus at the leadership level.

This was a talented executive team. They simply lacked clarity and alignment on what mattered most. This is far more common than you may realize.

Most leaders struggle to clearly articulate the strategy of their company. They can't explain how their company is going to win in the market. As such, most traditional strategy sessions confuse discussion with alignment.

You cannot march a team toward winning in the market if they don't clearly understand what winning looks like. Similarly, you cannot create real alignment with sticky notes and Sharpies.

This is exactly the kind of challenge AI can help you solve. Remember the Herbalife story at the opening of this chapter? Instead of one person talking at a time while everyone else waits, AI can interview every leader simultaneously. Instead of the loudest voices dominating, every voice is heard. Instead of walking out with the illusion of alignment, you walk out with a shared view of where you agree, where you don't, and what needs to happen next.

That is what strategic alignment looks like in an AI-driven organization.

The Quarterly Strategic Review

When I sit down with leader or an executive team to do a strategic review, we look at four key drivers of their business:

1. **Strategy:** Reviewing the competitive advantage you want to build in the long term through the actions you can take in the short term (your strategic plan).
2. **Execution:** Reviewing progress on your strategic plan and identifying what changes need to be made.
3. **People:** Ensuring you have the *right people* in the *right seats* doing the *right things* and growing in the *right direction.*
4. **Technology:** Evaluating how you can harness tech to help your people do higher-quality work in a fraction of the time, increase operational efficiency, and deliver more value to customers.

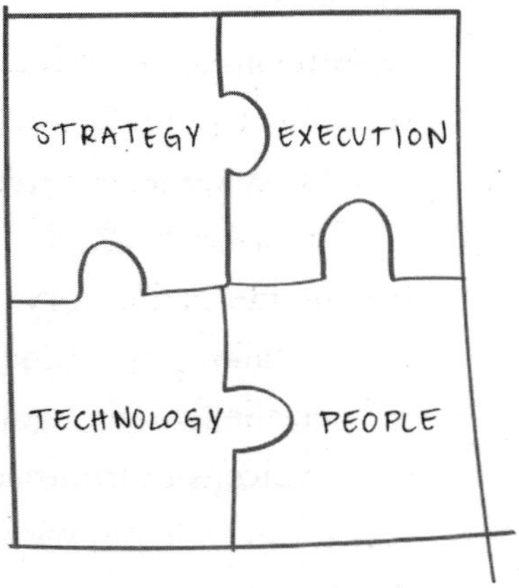

These four drivers provide the lens through which strategic clarity and alignment should be examined. When you look at your business through these four drivers, you can see where your strategy is clear and where it's fuzzy; where your people are aligned and where they're not; and where technology is accelerating progress and where it's being ignored.

This is not a tactical conversation. It is a high-level strategic discussion ensuring you are maximizing your people and technology to achieve your goals in alignment with the competitive advantage you want to build. Reviewing these four drivers allows you to make the necessary adjustments as markets and priorities shift and align your team so they can execute for the next quarter.

A quarterly review like this is valuable. It gives you a baseline cadence to pick your head up and make sure you're leading the company in the right direction. On its own, however, it is no longer enough. The world is moving too fast: priorities shift between quarters, and assumptions embedded in your plan may prove false before the quarter is over.

You need more than a quarterly check-in. You need a living structure that keeps your strategy current as reality changes. We'll get deeper into what that looks like in the next chapter.

Here are some initial questions you can ask yourself. The purpose of these is to help you clarify your thinking and align the four drivers—so you can clearly see what matters most. From there, you can identify the most important focus areas for the next quarter. I like to start with the traditional pen and paper and then turn to AI as my Thought Partner.

Strategy

1. What is the competitive advantage we are building in the long term?
2. What, if anything, has changed in the market since our last strategic review?
3. What have we learned from our customers that might better inform our strategy?

Execution

1. Where do we stand, goal versus actual, on our strategic plan? Where are we ahead of schedule and could consider raising our goal? Where have we fallen behind and need to make up the gap?
2. Are there new priorities that have surfaced that we need to account for? How should we prioritize them among the existing items on this plan?
3. If we say yes to adding something new, what are we deprioritizing?
4. What progress can we make between now and our next strategic review to ensure we are making sufficient progress toward our goals?
5. Who is responsible for delivering these results?

People

1. Do we have the *right people* in the *right seats* doing the *right things* and growing in the *right direction*?
2. Are they delivering results per their job description?
3. Are they acting in alignment with our culture?
4. What can I praise them for doing well?

5. What are the most important developmental goals they can achieve in the next ninety days to take their performance to the next level?
6. How can I clearly communicate this to them so they can improve in the next ninety days?
7. How can I adjust my leadership to help them grow to the next level?

Technology

1. What progress can we make in the next ninety days to help our people become AI-driven?
2. What are the most impactful ways we can engage technology to free our people up to do higher-value work?
3. Where do we have an operational bottleneck that if released, would make us more efficient?
4. Where do we have the opportunity to deliver more value to our customers with technology?
5. Based on this, what will we commit to implementing in the next ninety days?

I want to remind you that big changes start with small actions. If you are not used to asking questions like these, start small. Pick a few, and think deeply about them. Then identify the most important things you want to implement over the next quarter. It's not about implementing everything. It's about taking action on the most important things. Once I've done this initial round of thinking, I like to turn to my AI Thought Partner™ to enhance my thinking.

Harness AI to Enhance Your Quarterly Strategic Review

With you in the driver's seat as Thought Leader, engage AI as your

Thought Partner to interview you to help you clarify your thinking. Here is a basic prompt you can use to get started:

> Act as my Thought Partner and interview me with one question at a time to conduct a quarterly strategic review of my business. The questions should focus on these four drivers:
>
> 1. **Strategy:** What competitive advantage are we building in the long term through the actions we are taking in the short term?
> 2. **Execution:** What progress have we made toward our strategic plan so far this year? What changes do we need to make?
> 3. **People:** Are the right people in the right seats doing the right things and growing in the right direction?
> 4. **Technology:** How might we harness technology to help our people do higher-quality work in a fraction of the time, increase efficiency, and deliver more value to customers?
>
> Start with strategy and continue through each driver in order. Then give me feedback on what I'm doing well and where you see potential holes in my thinking, and list the top things I should consider focusing on in the next ninety days.

I strongly encourage you to try this prompt.

Few activities on your calendar this week will deliver as much value as this strategic review. To make this process even more impactful, use our AI Thought Partner™. It has been trained on the more detailed list of questions so it can facilitate your review. Scan this QR code or visit AiLeadership.com and say "help me do my quarterly strategy review."

Problem 3: Lack of an AI-Driven Execution System
Solution: Build a Living System That Turns Strategy Into Results

You've set a big goal, you have a plan in place to achieve it, and you've created real alignment across your leadership team. Now what?

This is where most plans break down.

If you're like most companies, you don't have a living system that ensures your strategy and plan stay up to date and actually turn into results. Your plan might live in a document on the CEO's computer or in the heads of a handful of leaders. The assumptions embedded in the plan are rarely tracked. Meanwhile, markets shift, priorities change, and roles evolve. But your plan? It remains static. This is because the systems you have in place were built for yesterday's work, and the tax to keep everything up to date is too high.

AI makes this even more complicated because it changes what people inside your company actually do. That means every role, workflow, system, and product or service will evolve.

What if the real source of value with AI wasn't identifying the right AI use cases, but building an AI-driven execution system that keeps strategy, people, and priorities moving together as the world changes?

Think about it this way. You need a structure that creates alignment, drives execution, keeps people accountable, and adapts as things change—because things will change. Goals evolve. Priorities shift. Markets move. Organizations get restructured.

Without a system to keep everything connected, alignment breaks down fast. What was clear starts to drift. What was aligned starts to fragment. And before you realize it, your plan is no longer driving results. Because plans don't go according to plan.

This is where AI changes the game.

AI can become the system that keeps everything connected. It can help you create clarity and alignment in a fraction of the time. It can track whether your assumptions still hold. It can surface when priorities need to shift. And it can help every person on your team focus on what matters most—this quarter, this month, this week—so they are consistently executing against the plan.

We'll go deeper into the mechanics of this in the next chapter, but the key takeaway from this chapter is simple: **your strategy must evolve as fast as the world around you.**

This is the work we now do with companies. We help leadership teams install an AI-driven execution system that keeps strategy, people, and priorities aligned as the business evolves—so they can turn strategy into results in a fraction of the time.

If you're facing a strategic challenge where the cost of misalignment is high, we collapse three to six months of alignment work into a matter of hours and begin installing the system to execute it.

To learn more, visit AiLeadership.com.

In the next chapter, I'll show you how to take the insights from your quarterly strategy review and turn them into focused action for the next thirty days, driving real results.

Here's the 20% from This Chapter

1. **Expand Who You Can Become:** The purpose of a goal is to expand who you and your organization can become. Set goals that require you to change how you think and act in order to achieve them.
2. **Create True Clarity and Alignment:** Real alignment involves shared understanding, surfaced assumptions, and genuine ownership. If your team can't clearly articulate how you're going to win in the market, you don't have alignment yet.
3. **Build an AI-Driven Execution System:** In an AI-driven world, strategy, roles, and priorities are changing too fast to rely on static plans alone. You need a living system that keeps strategy, people, and priorities moving together as reality changes.
4. **Use AI to Accelerate Alignment and Value Creation:** AI can help leaders hear every voice, surface what matters most, and move from conversation to commitment in a fraction of the time.
5. **Install Your System:** If you're ready to install an AI-driven execution system that turns your strategy into results in a fraction of the time, visit AiLeadership.com.

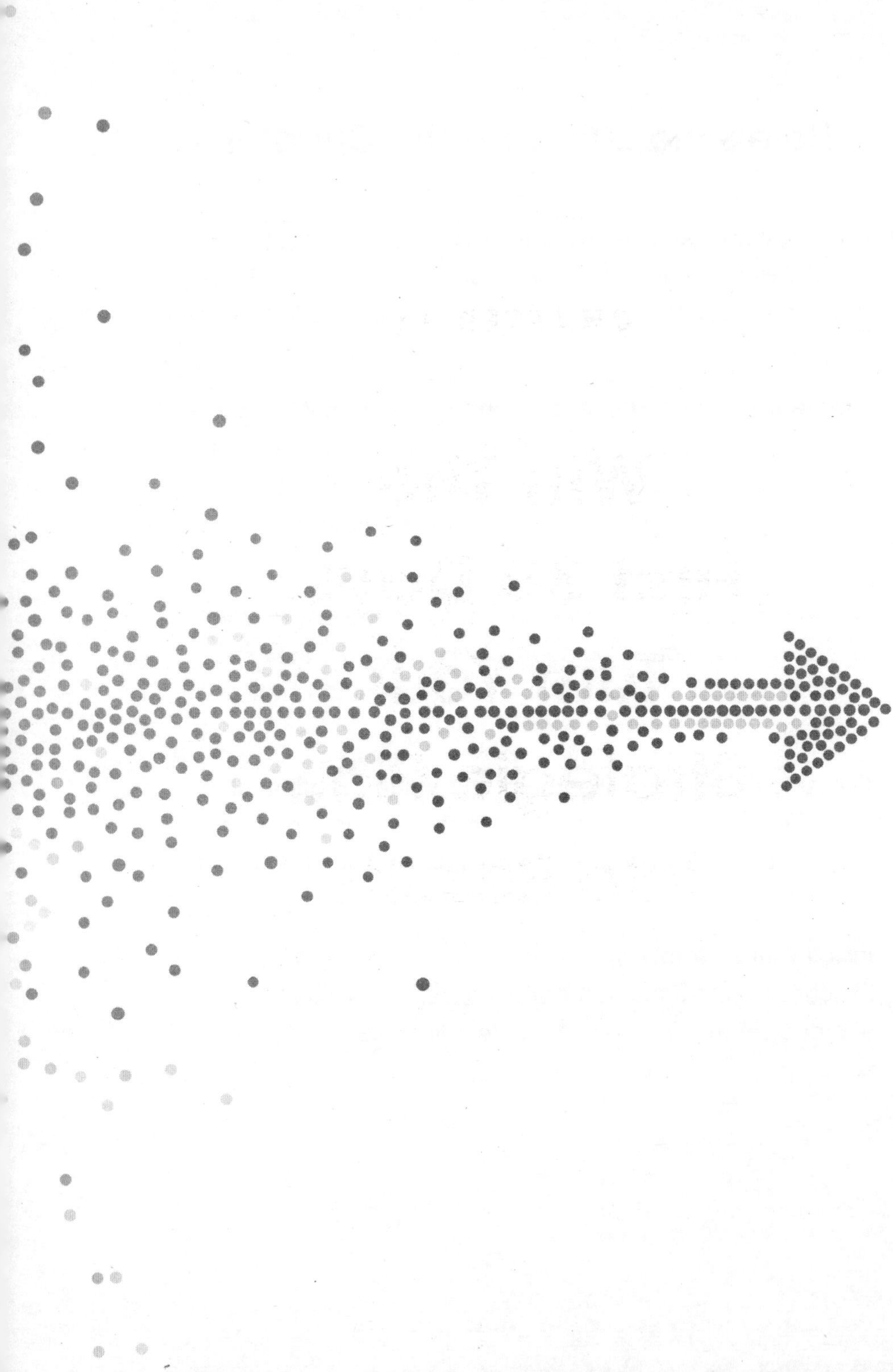

CHAPTER 11

Win The First 30 Days: Turn Your Strategic Plan Into Results

The year was 1911, and two teams were locked in a race against time, nature, and each other. The Norwegian team was led by Roald Amundsen and the British by Robert Falcon Scott. Both teams had their sights set on the same prize: being the first to plant their flag on the Geographic South Pole. Both teams had the same goal, but their strategies to reach it were as different as night and day.

The Norwegians had a meticulous plan and an unwavering determination to stick to it. No matter what Mother Nature threw their way, they pressed on, covering an impressive twenty miles every single day. Some days, the conditions were perfect—clear skies and favorable temperatures. Other days, it was as though the Antarctic itself was trying to stop them in their tracks, with blizzards, swirling winds, and blinding snowstorms that made it nearly impossible to see the way forward. But did the Norwegians let that stop them? Not a chance. They stayed in the driver's seat, marching forward twenty miles at a time, refusing to let the weather dictate their progress.

Then there was Robert Falcon Scott's British expedition. Their strategy was a bit different: cover as much ground as possible when the weather was good. But when conditions took a turn for the worse, they hunkered down and waited out the storm. Now, on the surface, this might seem like a smart move. Why risk the lives of your team when the climate was so brutal and unforgiving? But here's the problem: by letting the weather call the shots, they were essentially putting Mother Nature in the driver's seat and relegating themselves to the passenger seat.

The results of these two strategies couldn't have been more different. By staying in control and pushing forward no matter what, the Norwegian expedition reached the South Pole a full month ahead of the British team. When the British realized they'd lost the race, they turned back, following the same strategy of traveling when the weather was good and hunkering down when it wasn't. But this time, it cost them everything. They got caught in a deadly storm that claimed their lives.

As a leader, you face a similar struggle when it comes to executing your strategic plan. Your team is aligned and ready to put the plan into action, and then . . . it collides with reality.

Some weeks, it's like the conditions are perfect. Your calendar is wide open, and disruptions are minimal. It's the ideal scenario to stay focused on your 20% priorities—the ones that drive 80% of your results.

But then, in the blink of an eye, the climate can shift. Your days become like those relentless Antarctic blizzards. Customer issues crop up. Unexpected emergencies demand your attention. New initiatives get dropped on your plate. Strategic priorities that won't deliver immediate results but could elevate your future success get sidelined. Your carefully planned calendar is in shambles, and you find yourself reacting to everything that comes your way. It's like you are standing in the eye of the storm, just trying to figure out your next move. In those chaotic moments, it's easy to let the weather push you into the passenger seat, abandoning your plan to address the pressing matters that keep popping up.

But amid the chaos, there's a crucial question you need to ask yourself: who's in the driver's seat? You or Mother Nature? As an AI-driven leader, you know the answer. You stay in control.

It all comes down to prioritization. You have clarity on your plan. When things change and the storm hits, you have to ask yourself, "What matters most right now?" If you decide that making progress on your 20% march isn't as important as dealing with the storm, then you've made a conscious choice to prioritize the storm. That's okay. The key is to make it a choice, not a knee-jerk reaction.

But if the storm isn't your highest priority, stay focused on your plan, breaking it down into bite-sized milestones. Rain or shine, you make sure you're making progress on your 20% march. By committing to these short-term objectives, you take back control over your execution. You refuse to let the unpredictable forces of "Mother Nature" call the shots. It's that proactive stance that separates the leaders who forge ahead from those who end up stranded in the storm.

The actions you take in the first thirty days after your strategy review can make or break your results. These initial days are your launchpad, shaping the trajectory of your results and determining whether you'll succeed or fall short. It's during this crucial window that you have the chance to turn your strategic plan into actionable steps, mobilize your team, and ignite your progress.

But the importance of the first thirty days goes way beyond symbolism. This is your time to lead, set clear expectations, and show that AI-driven leaders stay in the driver's seat no matter what. When you do that, it inspires commitment from your team. By taking decisive action early on, you're sending a clear signal to your entire organization that you're committed to driving change and getting results.

In this chapter, we're going to explore how you can create a culture where you and your people stay in the driver's seat, turning your strategic plan into actionable milestones.

The Fundamentals of Effective Execution

You can have the most brilliant strategic plan and the highest-quality strategy review, but if you can't execute on it, it's not worth the paper it's printed on. Think about it like this: a strategic plan is like a roadmap. It shows you where you want to go and how to get there. But just having the map isn't enough. You need to actually get in the car and start driving. That's execution. Without it, you're just sitting in the driveway.

Effective execution comes down to a few key fundamentals:

1. Break Your Plan Down into Bite-Sized, Actionable

Milestones. These are the checkpoints that let you know you're on track and making progress.

2. **Block Off Time in Your Calendar to Take Action.** If you don't carve out dedicated time, it's all too easy to get sidetracked by the day-to-day fires that pop up.
3. **Create a Common Language** to discuss changes in priorities so you are responsive, not reactive, as things shift. This allows you to adapt to change while staying in the driver's seat and making progress toward your goals.
4. **Enhance the Value of Your One-on-Ones** by focusing the conversation on what will drive progress toward your goals and help them perform at higher levels.

Here's the kicker: many leaders struggle with at least one (if not all) of these fundamentals. When that happens it's like trying to drive cross-country with a flat tire. You are still moving forward, but it's slower and harder than it needs to be.

Let's look at some of the common challenges and obstacles that you might face when it comes to executing your plan.

Not Breaking Your Plan into Short-Term Milestones

Here's what often happens: leaders finalize their strategic plan, but then they miss a crucial step. They don't identify the specific progress that needs to be made in the next thirty days to ensure they start building momentum. Instead, they think, "I've got so much time to achieve my goals," so they get out of the gates at a modest pace. Then the storm hits. They hunker down, telling themselves they'll make up the gap later. They start to fall behind on their goals until one day, they look up and the gap is too big. So they give up on the goal. The truth is, the goal was never the issue. Their execution was. They allowed themselves to be in the passenger seat.

When you finalize your strategic plan or come out of a quarterly strategy review, invest the time to clarify the specific progress that needs to be made in the next thirty days.

We learned this firsthand. My company became customer zero for the AI-driven strategy execution system we built.

We realized that if we wanted to help other companies drive better execution with AI, we had to prove it worked on ourselves first. So we created a system that houses our entire annual business plan. It knows the role of every person on the team. As a Thought Partner, it asks each person the right questions to help them clarify priorities and understand what they need to accomplish by the end of the year, the quarter, the month, and the week.

This is what we now call the AI Thought Partner™—our AI-driven strategy execution system.

Thought Partner™ helps each person design their calendar that reflects a plan to achieve their goals—not just a list of meetings. Every week, it asks the right questions to help each person reprioritize and stay focused on what matters most. And when someone falls off track, it holds them accountable.

This transformed how our team executes. We stopped reviewing the plan once a quarter and hoping for the best because Thought Partner™ now keeps strategy alive every week.

Failing to Block Time

Every leader is interested in achieving their goals, but not all are truly committed. Want to know how I tell the difference? I ask to see their calendar.

Clarifying the actions you will take in the first thirty days is a great first step. But if your calendar does not have time blocked for those actions, it's wishful thinking. There are so many things scratching and clawing for your attention. It's way too easy to slip back into your old routine of reacting to what is most urgent rather than accomplishing what's most important. Gradually, you start falling behind on your plan and your goals.

"Every leader is interested in achieving their goals, but not all are truly committed. Want to know how I tell the difference? I ask to see their calendar."

Here's what I recommend: as soon as the strategic review is done and the actions for the first thirty days are clarified, open up your calendar and block the time you need to get those things done. By putting those time blocks in place, you're escalating your commitment to turning your plan into results. It also forces you to evaluate what matters most when your plan collides with the reality of a full calendar.

Here's a common mistake I want you to avoid: when you look at your calendar, don't just search for white space to block time. Many people do this, and they don't realize they are making all the existing appointments more important than the priorities they just identified. The truth is, your calendar should represent a plan to achieve your goals. Review the actions you need to take, and identify when you will be at your best to get them done. If there is something already scheduled, ask yourself, "What is more important: what's scheduled currently or this priority?" This is your time. You're going to have to say no to something. I want to make sure you say it to the right thing.

Want to take this even further? Give AI your thirty-day milestones and a screenshot of your calendar. Ask it to cross-reference the two. It will show you exactly where the gaps are; where your calendar is full of meetings that have nothing to do with your priorities, and where the time for your 20% march isn't protected. AI doesn't care that you've had a standing meeting with someone for two years. It just looks at what you said matters most and tells you whether your calendar reflects that. Do this every week, and you'll never have to wonder if you're in the driver's seat.

Lack of a Common Language around Prioritization

Want to know the telltale sign that your company doesn't have a common language around prioritization? When a new priority surfaces, most of the conversation is about the new item, not about what will be deprioritized to make room for it. Does this sound familiar?

Without this common language, here's what happens: you delegate to your people, and they say yes to the new item. It gets added to a list that already feels overwhelming. Then, they shift their focus from what they were working on to what's most recent or urgent. They start heading in a new direction.

Multiply this across every single person in your company. They're all on the same team, but they're constantly shifting their focus and heading in different directions at different times. On the surface, they might seem busy. In reality, they're not making the kind of coordinated progress that moves the needle. This is how you create a reactive culture.

No matter how good your strategic plan is, if you don't have a common language to discuss shifts in priorities, you'll never be fully aligned. You'll never row in the same direction. You will make reaching your destination harder.

I have two recommendations for you: one if you are a leader delegating to your people, and the other if your boss is delegating to you.

As the leader, when you delegate, state what you need help with, and then ask either of the following questions:

1. I need your help doing (insert the task). How would you prioritize this based on the other things on your plate?
2. I need your help doing (insert the task). Help me understand what you would be saying no to in order to say yes to this.

By following your request with one of those questions, you create a culture that understands when you say yes to one thing, you are saying no to everything else. It also gives you a window into how your people prioritize. This is a critical skill when it comes to developing them into strategic leaders. If you agree with their thinking, praise them. If you see it differently, guide them.

Here's what you can do if your boss is delegating to you. The best way to say no to your boss is by saying yes. Here's what this looks like.

Imagine your boss asks you to do something. You simply say, "I'd be happy to take that on. Based on what I have planned for the week, I would be able to get this to you by (share when you can have it done). Does that work for you?"

Now imagine they say they need it faster. You can say, "I can do that. To make sure we are aligned, here is what I would deprioritize to prioritize this. Does that work for you?"

Notice the entire time you remain in the driver's seat. You are educating your boss on the opportunity cost of switching from one priority to another. Your boss has the right to shift your priorities. Your job is to make it an educated decision.

To start creating a common language around prioritization, stop talking about items as though they exist in a vacuum. Start talking about how they fit in the context of all the other things on your plate and which will make the biggest impact toward your goals.

Ineffective One-On-Ones

A lot of leaders have regular one-on-ones with their direct reports, but I often find they don't have a clear structure to maximize the impact of their time together. Many times, those conversations are just project updates. For some leaders, it's a chance to dump even more things on their people's plates.

I suggest you take a different approach. If you believe that the best way to achieve your goals is for your people to focus on what matters most, then focus your conversations on that! Ask great questions to evaluate if they are making the progress they expect to be making. How clear are they on what matters most this week? Are they prioritizing so the most important things get sufficient space on their calendars? What are the distractions that are threatening their focus? How can you support them? Where do you see opportunities for them to perform at an even higher level? How can you guide them there?

When you approach your one-on-ones with this kind of mindset, you will find this quickly becomes one of the most impactful meetings you have during the week. My question for you is this: who would you have to become to make this your reality? You get to decide if this is "another idea" you read in a book or something you implement in your business.

By putting these strategies into action, you ensure that your strategic plan isn't just a pretty document but a roadmap for real results. Set monthly milestones, block time for your priorities, create a common language to discuss shifts in priorities, and enhance your weekly one-on-ones. This is how you empower yourself and your team to execute with laser focus and achieve your goals.

Strategically Harness AI to Drive Enhanced Execution

You're ready to take focused action on a monthly basis toward your strategic plan. It's time to supercharge your thinking with AI to kick your execution into overdrive.

When I was with Jindal Steel & Power, one of our subsidiary businesses was in need of a big turnaround. Up till this point, the business reported to the managing director of Jindal Steel & Power. However, the MD needed to focus elsewhere, so the chairman asked this business to start reporting to me instead.

One month, the CEO sent me the board deck. I opened it up, and what did I find? Sixty-six pages of detailed information and only a few hours to go before our board meeting. I dove in and reviewed it the best I could with the time I had, jotting down my list of questions for the CEO. Then, a lightbulb went off in my head. "How might AI help me do this?"

I had the necessary privacy provisions in place, so I felt good about uploading the deck to AI. I wrote the following prompt:

> I want you to act as an aggressive growth-minded board member with deep expertise in company turnarounds. Attached is the board deck for this business. It's not doing well and needs to be turned around. I'd like you to identify the top five questions that you would be asking the CEO during this meeting. Please list them in order of priority, as we only have one hour for the review, and I want to make sure I'm asking the most important questions first.

I hit enter. Instantly, it spit out five questions. As I reviewed them, I realized that four of the questions it generated were ones I had already written down. But one question was something I missed.

> Production was 20,000 tons below the projections for October. The cost of production was higher than planned, leading to a loss of $90 per tonne. What is the root cause of this, and what strategies are we putting in place to ensure this does not happen in the future?

What a great question! It was aligned with our goals and clear, and it provoked deeper thinking.

I realized this question was the most important one I could ask. I showed up for the board meeting and thanked the CEO for the deck. Then I fired off that question. When I asked it, the CEO's eyes got huge. He looked at me and said, "Wow, you really did go through the deck." I just smiled at him and waited for his response.

It's tough to read the label when you're inside the box. Business is complicated enough. Constantly tracking and measuring your progress towards your goals and figuring out what you need to do to get there can be overwhelming. This is where AI can play a valuable role as your Thought Partner. Here are four prompts you can use to apply what we covered in this chapter:

Turning Your Strategic Plan into Thirty-Day Milestones

> Attached is our strategic plan. The next step is to identify the specific progress we need to make for each item on the plan in the next thirty days to be on track for our targets. Ask me one question at a time to help gather this information, and then generate an executive summary I can send to my team so we are aligned.

Restructuring Your Calendar so It Reflects a Plan for Your Goals

> Here are my top priorities for this week: (List your top priorities). Here is also a picture of my calendar for the week. In reviewing my calendar, I don't feel it reflects a clear plan to achieve my weekly goals. Acting as the Interviewer, ask me one question at

a time to help me identify changes I can make to the calendar.

Once we're done with the review, I want you to help draft the communication I need to send to the people I'm canceling or rescheduling.

Creating a Common Language of Prioritization

I am the leader of a business. Historically, I've delegated to people by simply adding things to their plate but rarely having conversations about subtracting. As a result, I'm concerned people are reacting to what's most recent and losing focus on what's most important.

I'd like you to act as an executive coach by asking me one question at a time to help me think through how I might change what I say and ask when I delegate. Success would be describing what I need them to take on and then shifting the conversation to where they believe this falls in order of priority. This will ensure they do not react and always stay focused on what matters most.

Enhancing the Value of Your One-on-Ones

Acting as my Thought Partner, help me identify three to five questions I can bring to my next series of one-on-ones with my direct reports. My goal is to act as a great coach, focusing our conversation on:

1. Ensuring they are clear on where their focus needs to be

this week to drive progress toward our thirty-day milestones.

2. Helping them think through the challenges they might encounter this week and how to proactively address them.
3. Raising their performance this week so they continue to develop and grow.

Ask me one question at a time to gather the information you need, and then generate a list of questions for me to consider.

These prompts are designed to get you started. For a more comprehensive list of prompts, check out the appendix section of the book. I've included the prompts above as well as prompts to have AI be your Thought Partner in analyzing the trade-offs in priorities when things change, turning monthly milestones into weekly priorities, discovering how to say no to your boss, and still be a team player, and many more.

If you want to really drive this in your company, check out the AI Thought Partner™ at AiLeadership.com. It's built to be the AI-driven strategy execution system for your business; it houses your plan and helps each leader prioritize and execute week after week. Scan this QR code or visit AiLeadership.com to get started.

The tale of Amundsen and Scott's race to the South Pole is a stark reminder: a plan is just words without focused, consistent action. In business, a plan, no matter how grand, will inevitably collide with reality. It's a truth I've witnessed repeatedly in my work with executive teams. No plan unfolds as devised. Changes happen. Mistakes occur. Unexpected events pop up. Not anticipating the unpredictable is a recipe for failure. The key is to keep marching forward.

In the next chapter, you will learn how to create an environment that encourages strategic thinking at every level. You will discover how to 10x the impact of every employee.

Here's the 20% from This Chapter

1. The actions you take in the first thirty days after your strategic review can make or break your goals. Get out of the gates fast, and build a lead in your first thirty days.
2. There are four simple steps you can take to drive execution of your strategic plan:
    1. Break your plan down into small, actionable milestones.
    2. Have time blocked on your calendar to take those actions. Your calendar is not set in stone. If you don't have time to focus on your priorities, cancel things that are less important.
    3. Create a common language around prioritization so people can discuss what matters most and keep rowing in the same direction.
    4. Elevate the impact of your one-on-ones by coaching your people to focus on what matters most each week and helping them perform at an even higher level.

CHAPTER 12

10x the Impact of Every Employee

Four months into the job, my executive assistant Marianella was exceeding every expectation I had for her. She was crushing it, which meant it was time to raise our goals for the impact she could make inside our company.

I sat down with her in one of our weekly one-on-ones. I told her how well she was doing and gave her a challenge: **"I want you to cast a vision for how you can bring ten to one hundred times more value to AI Leadership. Use AI. Write CRIT™. Have it interview you about your core strengths, and figure out how to focus those on the priorities of your role in alignment with the company's goals. Then, use AI to turn those strengths into superpowers."**

She said, "Got it," and we went on our way. Now, to be clear, before working with me, Marianella knew how to spell AI—but that was about it. She had never used any of the large language models. She literally read this book, and I taught her how to write CRIT™.

She came back to me the next week and said, "I'm ready."

I asked her, "With what?"

She said, "My vision."

"Based on my strengths," she said, "here's the 20% I'm currently doing that I need to double down on because it will bring ten times more value. Here are all the things I'm not doing that, based on my strengths, I really should be doing because they will enable me to bring ten times more value. But if I'm going to focus on those things, here's everything I'm currently doing that I will have to stop doing."

She divided the stop list into groups: things we should stop doing altogether because they don't bring value, things AI could augment or automate so they still get done without a human, and things that still need a human. Then she said, "Based on this, here's the job description for my replacement. Here are their 20% priorities, a ninety-day onboarding plan, and research on compensation ranges. Based on that, I recommend we pay them $X. Do I have your permission to move forward?"

I was floored. After praising her, she said, "Thank you, but we're not done yet."

"You didn't just ask me to cast a vision for ten times more value," she said. "You asked for ten to one hundred times more value."

I sat back in my chair. Whatever was coming next was going to be good. She continued, "My biggest realization is that there's no way I can bring one hundred times more value to the company unless I make you one hundred times more valuable."

I was speechless. She had architected a prompt so AI would interview me to identify how I could bring one hundred times more value to the company.

I said, "I can't wait to do this."

She said, "Good. Do it now. I'll wait."

So she waited while AI interviewed me.

It generated a vision for how I could bring one hundred times more value to the company, along with a system of rules we would have to embed to transform how I allocate my time. I told her it was one of the most valuable prompts I'd ever done.

She said, "I appreciate that, but we have a problem. I can put these rules in place, but you love to break the rules. So I've taken the liberty of creating one more prompt that will interview you to identify every way you might try to get around these rules—and build a defense system. That way, if you ever want to break a rule, you'll have to go through AI first."

This fundamentally transformed how I allocate my time—and the impact I make in my company.

You tell me, do you think Marianella is at least ten times more impactful? Absolutely. I promoted her. She moved from being my executive assistant, focused on my inbox, calendar, and 80% tasks, to becoming our Executive Multiplier and Advisory Lead for LATAM. Her role shifted to making me one hundred times more impactful, leading our advisory engagements in Latin America, and running our rhythm of the business and culture processes.

Marianella did not have to become an AI expert. She simply became an AI-driven leader. She read this book, wrote CRIT™, and used AI in a strategic way. Might it be possible that you too have an opportunity to expand what's possible for the people inside your organization? This is exactly the kind of potential your team can unlock with AI, unleashing levels of value and innovation you never thought possible.

History teaches us that technological breakthroughs shift the value of human skills. Those who are able to harness the technology to empower their people drive greater growth. As an AI-driven leader, you have the opportunity to capitalize on this shift and 10x the impact of every employee. In this chapter, I will show you how you can do this by:

1. Harnessing the strengths of your people, focusing on the priorities of their roles, and aligning with your company's goals.
2. Supercharging their efforts with AI to achieve higher-quality work in less time.
3. Streamlining and automating the 80% low-value tasks to free up more of their time.
4. Establishing new standards for performance to take them to the next level.

Focus on the 20% Priorities of the Role

I used to make all the mistakes when hiring. I thought a job description was a comprehensive list of everything the role required, so I'd spend a lot of time capturing everything. After posting the job, I'd interview candidates, asking questions based on their resumes and whatever was on my mind. Once I found someone I liked, I'd hire them. On their first day, we'd review the role, and they'd start working. Over time, I'd delegate tasks to them as needed. Eager to impress, they'd always say yes and take on more. Fast forward three to six months, and they were overwhelmed and underperforming. I'd think, "They must not be the right person for the job." But the problem was my leadership.

If this situation sounds familiar, you are not alone. Many leaders hire people for their potential but then struggle to give them the clear direction they need to succeed. To make matters worse, most leaders won't take the time to uncover the unique strengths of each candidate. This can lead to situations where you're effectively hiring a surgeon to mow your lawn. Yes, they can do the job, but their most valuable skills are wasted.

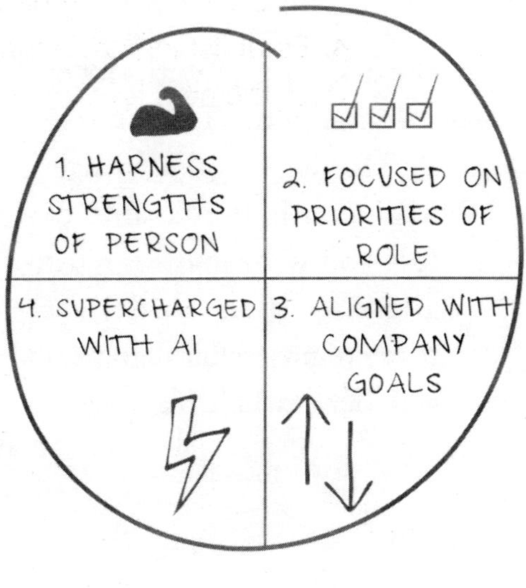

I don't look at job descriptions as a laundry list of everything a person needs to do anymore. Not everything is equally important to achieving our goals. Now, I focus on what will allow each employee to 10x their impact.

In *10x Is Easier Than 2x®*, Dan Sullivan and Dr. Benjamin Hardy share a powerful idea: You can double your growth by letting go of 20% of what you do. But if you want to hit that coveted 10x growth, you've got to let go of 80% of what you do to free yourself up to move to higher-level activities.

If you want to 10x the impact of every employee, it will take more than just equipping them with a ChatGPT account. You'll need to adopt this mentality: 20% of their role drives 80% of the results. It's your job to zero in on that 20%.

Here's how I do it with new hires. First, I define the 20% of the role that will drive 80% of the results in alignment with our company goals. For example, I hired a VP of Operations. Their 20% was to:

1. Turn my vision into plans into results
2. Build and lead a high-performance team
3. Build systems for scale without slowing the company down

Then when I interview a candidate, I use my questions to validate if they can perform in the 20%. When I onboard a new hire, I outline a clear ninety-day plan for what they need to do to be successful delivering results in those critical 20% areas.

Anytime I delegate a task to someone on my team, I hold it up against their 20% and ask, "Is this a priority or a distraction?" This simple shift has been a game changer. My team is better able to focus on what matters most, allowing them to deliver better results in full alignment with our strategic plan.

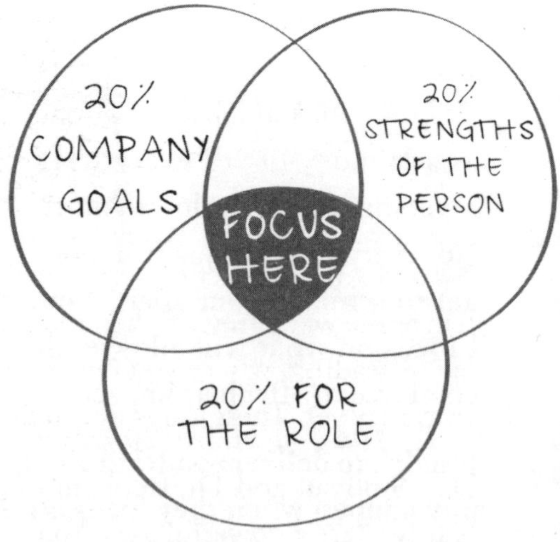

Here are some questions you can ask to evaluate opportunities to increase the impact of your people:

1. Based on our strategic plan, what are the 20% priorities that will drive 80% of our results this year at a company level?
2. If I had to rewrite the job description for this position, what would be the 20% priorities our goals would require this role to do exceptionally well?
3. Who is occupying that role? What are their greatest strengths that could drive 80% of the impact they could make?
4. Am I fully leveraging their strengths in their current role?
5. What changes can I make based on these insights?

I also encourage you to ask yourself these questions for your role. We've built this directly into our AI Thought Partner™. Simply scan the QR code, and it will begin interviewing you, guiding you to uncover your strengths, clarify your priorities, and align them with your company's goals.

To 10x the impact of every employee, you have to fundamentally change the way you view their jobs. You have to let go of the industrial way of leading, where you delegate things and expect your team to always say yes. **Their job is not to do everything on their job description. It's to deliver results in alignment with your culture. That will only happen when they focus on the 20% that drives the majority of the results.**

Supercharge Your People's Impact with AI

I had the chance to demonstrate the power of AI while interviewing an executive for this book. When she asked what it looks like to become AI-driven, I drew the AI Empowerment Curve:

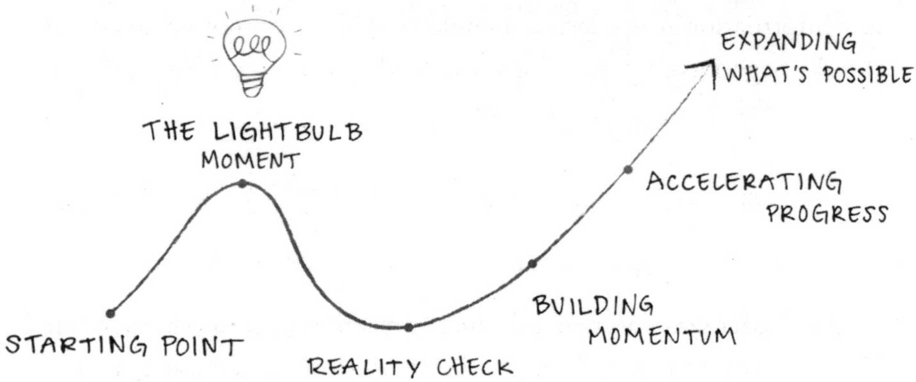

I explained that she was at the starting point, where she had both optimistic and skeptical views about AI. Her first step was to have a lightbulb moment where she would experience AI turn a relatable moment into a remarkable experience.

She looked confused and asked what that would look like. I asked her to describe a current challenge where having a Thought Partner would be valuable. She mentioned a personnel issue: a rock star performer who was toxic from a cultural standpoint. She was conflicted on what to do.

I told her this was a great use case for AI as a Thought Partner and began writing a prompt:

> I'm a leader with a personnel issue and need HR advice . . .

She interrupted, "Wait, you can do that?"

I smiled and said, "Oh yeah!" and continued typing, outlining the situation she had described. I asked her what she had done in the past. She sighed, explaining that every time she tried to talk to the employee about their attitude, they got defensive and flustered. The employee was a huge drag on the team, but she couldn't afford to lose them and wasn't sure what to do.

We shared this with AI, and instructed it to interview her to gather any information it needed so it could provide a recommendation. As the AI began asking questions, the leader responded. Then, the AI dropped this bomb of a question:

> It seems like you know what you should do. What are you afraid of?

The leader was stunned. AI's question hit her like a hammer. She looked at me and said, "I know what I need to do. They've got to go. We will figure out how to make up the gap."

This was her lightbulb moment. This situation had been weighing on her for months. But by harnessing AI as her Thought Partner, she was able to clarify her thinking and make a decision in less than five minutes. She was excited and couldn't wait to see what else AI could do.

This is what your people will experience. Once they have their lightbulb moment, they will feel excited to start trying AI more regularly. Manage their expectations that they are about to have a reality check. AI won't consistently deliver quality results, and they might wonder if they are wasting their time. The problem isn't AI; it's the way they are communicating with AI. When they hit the reality check, get curious and ask, "How might I improve my communication with AI?" If they focus on using better communication ingredients, they will get better results. They will be building momentum.

As AI delivers more value, encourage them to expand its use

beyond strategic thinking to decision-making, drafting communication, analyzing reports, or conducting research. At this point, their goal is to explore AI's limits and how to communicate effectively with it.

As they get more comfortable using AI across various use cases, they will be accelerating progress, achieving higher-quality work in less time. Suddenly their work will shift from being the master of their role to being a composer of strategy and a conductor of teams and technology.

Eventually, they will start to see possibilities where they only saw problems before. They will ask questions they never thought to ask and challenge assumptions that held them back. This is the power of becoming AI-driven. It will expand your thinking, challenge your beliefs, and help you become a better version of yourself.

Streamlining and Automating the 80%

Many leaders wonder how AI might make their people and operations more efficient by automating their processes. Elon Musk would suggest this is the *last thing* you should be asking. If you really want to free your people up from 80% of their tasks, you have to start by thinking differently.

In the biography of Elon Musk, Walter Isaacson detailed Elon's five rules for process improvement. These simple rules are the reason Elon and his teams were able to create reusable rockets at a fraction of the cost previously imaginable. These rules also led to many of the tech enhancements that make driving a Tesla so remarkable.

In this section, we're going to use Elon's five rules to help us with streamlining and automating the 80%. (Remember earlier in the chapter, when I suggested your team should set aside 80% of their tasks? That's the focus here.)

The first step is to question every requirement. In business today, there are many things we do without understanding why. As a result, we continue doing things certain ways because that's the way they've always been done. This is not where innovation lies.

If you want to liberate yourself and your team from the 80% low-value tasks and cumbersome processes, you have to be willing to challenge every assumption. In his companies, Elon requires that you never accept a requirement for a product without questioning where it came from, why it's there, and if it makes sense to you.

Once you have a better understanding of why the requirement exists, the second step is to delete any part of the process you can. Within his companies, Musk has a rule that you have to strip away 80% of the requirements for a product. He even says that if you don't have to add 10% back, then you're not cutting deep enough.

I experienced the result of this the first time I drove a Tesla. My wife and I landed at Newark Airport to celebrate our ten-year wedding anniversary. We got into our rental car, a Tesla Model 3. For the first three minutes, my wife and I were looking for the start button. It didn't exist! After firing up YouTube, we learned that you simply lay the key down on the flat surface by the cup holders between the driver's and passenger seat and step on the brake. Instantly, the car turned on.

As we began driving, I let off the accelerator, and the car slowed to an accelerated stop. I thought the emergency brake was on, but I couldn't find it. Again, we went back to YouTube. That was when I learned about regenerative braking. Someone designing the vehicle challenged the assumption that you should have to step on a brake for the car to stop. Simply by releasing your foot off the accelerator, the car will begin stopping itself.

We drove from Newark Airport over two hours through New York's bumper-to-bumper traffic to Washington, Connecticut. I didn't touch the brake once. This blew my mind.

When we pulled up to our resort and parked the car, I realized

I didn't know how to turn the car off or lock it. There was no button for either. Back to YouTube again. I discovered the way you turn the car off is by simply getting out of it. And the way you lock it is by shutting the door and holding your rental key up to the door.

Most cars today have a physical key or on/off button, require you to brake to slow down, need to be turned off manually, and must be locked when you exit. Why? Because that's the way it's always been done.

Our thinking drives our actions, which drive our results. If you want to 10x the value of every employee, you have to break the old ways of thinking, of assuming the 80% has to get done, and challenge whether it needs to be done at all.

As an AI-driven leader, you start by asking:

1. What is the importance of this task?
2. How does this help us or distract us?
3. Can we stop doing it?

This alone will begin to free people up. This is when we go to Elon's third step: simplify and optimize. The mistake many leaders make is they try to simplify and optimize things that shouldn't exist to begin with. Assuming you've questioned why something exists and deleted as much as you can, then you earn the right to ask, "How might we make this simpler?"

Assuming you've simplified as much as possible, then you go to the fourth step by asking, "How might we accelerate the process so the same amount can be done in less time?"

Then and only then should you ask, "How might we automate this?" which is the fifth and final step.

Elon Musk's Five Steps for Process Improvement

1. Question every requirement.
2. Delete any part of the process you can.
3. Simplify and optimize.
4. Accelerate.
5. Automate.

By following these steps, you'll start to free your people up from the low-value 80% tasks that stop them from making the biggest impact. This will allow them to reinvest their time in higher-value priorities.

Streamlining and automation are regular topics of discussion with the companies we advise. Throughout the year, leaders have breakthroughs while using technology to free up their teams. When someone discovers a solution, they share it with their organization and the impact compounds. This collaborative approach means you don't have to navigate these changes alone

I encourage you to do the same thing within your organization. Think big in terms of the change you want to make, and start with the small actions you can take. Identify one to three potential use cases, and evaluate the impact of freeing your people up from these. Take action if it makes sense. Then share what you learn with others. We'll dive deeper into the criteria you should consider in the next chapter.

But for now, let this sink in: by harnessing AI to enhance your people's impact and streamlining the 80%, you're not just making your organization more efficient. You're creating a culture where people are empowered to do their best work, to focus on what truly matters, and to continuously push the boundaries of what's possible.

With that in place, it's time to raise your standards for performance.

Thinking Leverage: Setting a New Standard that Elevates Performance

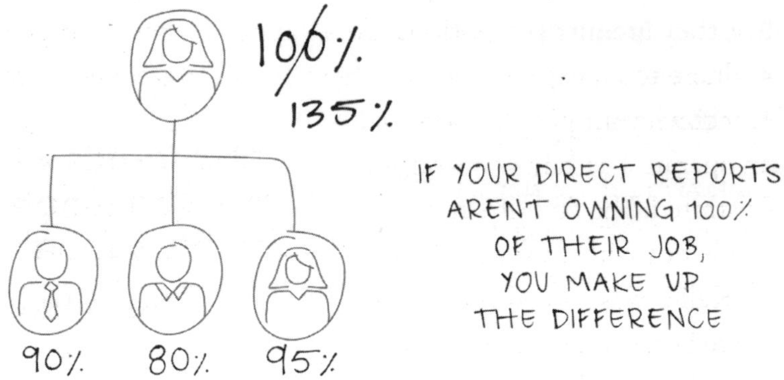

In the above figure, you're sitting at the top of your organizational chart, responsible for owning 100% of your job. You don't get to pass the buck to anyone else. It's *your* job. Below you are your three direct reports. The first only owns 80% of their job. The second owns 90%, and the third owns 95%. Where do the missing percentages go? Right back to you.

Suddenly, not only are you doing 100% of your job, but you're also taking on an additional 35% of the work your team should be doing. You find yourself working longer hours, burning out, and sacrificing your personal life. Who's fault is this? I used to think it was my people's. What I learned was that the fault was mine. I had trained my people that it was okay to not own 100% of their job because when they fell short, I would pick up the slack and save them. If this resonates with you, there is good news. You have the power to change this situation.

To do so, you have to understand the two primary reasons we end up taking pieces of our people's jobs:

Reason 1: Having Suggestions instead of Standards

You have expectations for how you want your people to perform. The problem arises when you think your expectations are standards, when in reality, they are just suggestions. This happens when your people do not adhere to an expectation and there are no consequences from you. Over time, your people learn that they can operate a certain way, and you grow frustrated. The fault lies not with your people but with your leadership.

> **"Standards without consequences are merely suggestions."**
> **—Gene Rivers**

Gary Keller was a great role model for me here because, on day 1, he made it clear that the best part about my job was it was *my* job! If I tried to give him pieces of my job, I would no longer have one.

Reason 2: Lack of Trust and Patience

Have you ever found yourself in a situation where instead of asking a member of your team how they would approach a problem, you just told them what to do? We've all been there. The problem with this approach is that thinking is part of their job, and by doing it for them, you're undermining their role.

If you examine the reasons behind this, it's because you either thought it would be faster to give them the answer, or you didn't trust that they could come up with a solution as good as yours. The result is that your people never develop the thinking skills required to reach your level and eventually succeed you.

Think about your children taking their first steps. What would happen if, the first time they tried to take a step, you swept them off the ground and carried them to their destination because "it would be faster" or "you could do it better than them"? When it comes to raising children, we understand that we cannot do everything for them. Great parenting involves helping your kids struggle well. A healthy struggle requires two things: a safe environment and support.

The same lessons apply to developing your people at work. Your job is not to do everything for them but to create opportunities for healthy struggle. Your focus should be on providing a safe environment and support to build the skills they need to succeed at the next level. As the value of human work shifts from operational to strategic, create opportunities for healthy struggle when it comes to strategic thinking.

Ask them questions, and give them the space to search for an answer. The goal is not for them to have the right answer immediately but for them to learn how to arrive at the right answer independently.

When you ask them questions, you gain insight into their thought process. This helps you identify their current ability to think strategically and determine where they can improve. Then, you can coach them to reach the next level. This shift moves you away from a culture where people wait to be told what to do toward a future where they proactively contribute ideas, solve problems, and help achieve your shared goals. Not only will this free you up at an executive level, but it also begins to develop succession candidates for your role, allowing you to move to the next opportunity when the time is right.

To truly 10x the impact of every employee, start by ensuring people own 100% of their roles, including thinking leverage. Remember, it's strategy first; technology second.

Three Ways to Enhance Your Team's Thinking Leverage

1. ASK MORE; GIVE LESS

Your people come to you with their questions because you have trained them to. When they ask, you give them the answer. If and when this happens, you may eventually find yourself wondering why your people don't do enough independent thinking and always come to you for the answer. It's simple. You trained them to. If you want this to change, it starts with you.

The first step is to become aware of how often you give your people answers instead of asking them questions and evaluating their thinking.

I once had a coach who used to close his office door when he was in meetings. On the door, he would have a piece of paper with three questions that people had to answer before knocking:

1. What's your name?
2. What's your question?
3. What are three potential solutions?

Pretty quickly, people stopped knocking on his door and started solving their own problems.

I learned this lesson firsthand when I walked into Jay's office with a question. He responded, "Geoff, my job as a leader is to teach you how to think. I have an answer, but I'm not going to give it to you yet. What do you think you should do?"

The more you ask, the more thinking leverage your people will bring you.

2. EXPLAIN WHY

Of course, there are moments when it is appropriate to give your people answers. In those moments, simply follow up your answer with,

"Here's why I'm suggesting this . . ." so you can teach them how to think at your level.

I remember a time when our head of learning and development for Jindal Steel came to me with a dilemma. She was supporting me on an important initiative but had several other departments with competing requests. She simply had more on her plate than she could accomplish in the time that remained. When she came to me, it was clear that she had done her own thinking. She knew what she should do, but internal politics put her in a tricky situation. She didn't need questions; she needed guidance.

First, I told her my recommendation for what to prioritize and what to deprioritize. Then, I followed my answer up with, "Here's why I'm suggesting this . . ."

3. BRING CONSEQUENCES TO STANDARDS NOT MET

What should you do if someone continues to not bring the level of thinking leverage required for the role? Impose consequences.

A consequence does not have to be a punishment. It can be as simple as a conversation. When onboarding a new assistant, I explained to her that a big part of her job was bringing me thinking leverage. That meant that when it came to the things in her job description, she needed to think through how to solve problems first before asking me what to do.

I remember the first time she came to me with a question that I thought she could have answered. I simply said, "You may not realize it, but you are asking me to do your thinking for you. You are an incredibly smart person, and I know you can think this through. What do you think you should do?"

There was no frustration in my tone. It was empathetic, yet firm. At that moment, she walked me through her thinking, which was sound. I then praised her for thinking it through. I affirmed that I thought she was thinking about it correctly and reinforced that when she has a question, I first want her to think through how she might approach it. Then, if she wants, she can come to me for coaching by stating the situation and how she plans to tackle it. She can then invite my perspective.

What do you do if you have this conversation and they continue to fall below the standard? This is when consequences need to become more direct. You might say, "On several occasions recently, you have come to me with questions that I believe you could have solved yourself. I want you to know that this does not meet our standard when it comes to thinking leverage for your role. I believe you are capable of exceeding the standard. Can you help me understand what's preventing you from meeting it? What support do you need from me? My expectation moving forward is that if you have a question, you need to first present the situation and what you think you should do, and then you are welcome to ask for my feedback."

When you hold thinking leverage up as the new standard, your people will rise to meet and exceed it. If they do not, then you can evaluate whether they are in the right role.

Your people are one of your greatest investments. The problem is, the industrial way of working has created a reality where your people spend most of their time on low-value tasks. AI is a catalyst for change—and the opportunity to automate so much of what is done today. Harness the strengths of your people, focused on the priorities of their roles, aligned with company goals, then supercharge them with AI to 10x their impact.

In the next chapter, we will discuss how you can seamlessly integrate AI with change management strategies that will create a smooth transition.

Here's the 20% from This Chapter

1. To 10x the impact of every employee, start by aligning the strengths of a person with the most important parts of their role and the goals of the organization. Then supercharge them with AI.
2. Streamline and automate the 80% over time. Empower people to ask *why* something has to be done and to remove things if possible. If not, empower them to simplify them, explore ways to do them faster, and finally consider automating them.
3. Moving from operational to strategic means enforcing a new standard with your people that they own 100% of their role, including thinking leverage.
4. Many leaders think they have standards when they really have suggestions. This is because when people do not adhere to the expectation, there is no consequence.

CHAPTER 13

Integrate AI Seamlessly: Change Management Strategies for Smooth Transitions

In the mid-2000s, Domino's Pizza had fallen on hard times. Despite being one of the most recognized pizza chains globally, they faced declining sales, dissatisfied customers, and a tarnished reputation.

Then in January 2008, Domino's launched their pizza delivery tracker to boost online sales and enhance the customer experience. Initially, the results were promising: the Pizza Tracker helped increase online ordering profits by 23%, and online sales jumped from less than 15% to 20% of total sales. But the problem was overall sales were still declining. Why? Their pizza sucked!

Focusing on convenience and marketing only highlighted Domino's poor product. Customer reviews were scathing, describing the pizza as tasting like cardboard and criticizing the use of frozen and canned ingredients. This situation reached a boiling point when a video showing Domino's employees contaminating food went viral on YouTube. The company's mishandled crisis response only worsened the situation, with their attempt to label the incident a "hoax." Public confidence in the brand plummeted.

A turnaround was desperately needed. Enter Patrick Doyle, Domino's CEO at the time. In the company's 2009 *Pizza Turnaround* video, he said, "You can either use negative comments to get you down, or you can use them to excite you and energize your process to make a better pizza." He chose the latter.

To turn the company around, Doyle focused on one thing: transparency. Domino's wasn't just going to claim their pizza had improved. They were going to prove it. Leadership understood that transparency couldn't just be a marketing campaign. They knew it had to be woven into the company's DNA.

As CEO, Doyle's job was to be the composer of strategy—casting the vision for transparency as the competitive advantage that would rebuild trust. To bring that vision to life, he tapped Russell Weiner, then CMO and now Domino's CEO, to be the conductor of teams and technology.

In my interview with Russell Weiner for this book, he shared how he got in the driver's seat and worked with his team to align every aspect of the business around transparency. The first step was fixing the product itself. Domino's reinvented its recipe from the ground up, eliminating frozen and canned ingredients and replacing them with fresh dough, a bolder sauce, and high-quality cheese. But Weiner knew that simply claiming the pizza had improved wouldn't be enough. Customers had to see the change with their own eyes.

To reinforce this, Domino's redesigned its stores to remove the barriers between customers and the kitchen. Instead of an enclosed back room, the new layout allowed people to watch their pizzas being made in real time, turning what was once a closed-off process into an open, transparent experience.

Technology played a crucial role in reinforcing this new identity. The Pizza Tracker became a centerpiece, allowing customers to follow their order step by step, from preparation to delivery. To further prove their commitment to transparency, Domino's did something unheard of at the time: they displayed live customer feedback in stores and online, unfiltered and in real-time. This move sent a clear message, Domino's was done hiding.

Even their marketing strategy was built on this foundation. Instead of relying on flashy promotions or price discounts, Domino's ran a brutally honest campaign, publicly admitting that their pizza had been terrible and showing the transformation step by step. Transparency wasn't just a response to criticism; it became a competitive advantage.

This commitment to transparency extended beyond the store experience it shaped every decision the company made. Once Domino's had built trust with customers, they doubled down on making ordering as seamless and accessible as possible.

In 2011, the company launched their iPhone app. In the first month, the app did $1 million in sales. After ninety days, it was doing $1 million a week. By 2022, over 91% of Domino's sales came from their digital channels, and average order value had increased. They formed strategic partnerships so customers could place orders using Amazon Echo and Apple Watch—while 75% of the U.S. restaurant industry was still struggling to launch functional apps.

Ultimately, it wasn't just the pizza or the technology that turned Domino's around—it was leadership. With Doyle composing the strategy and Weiner conducting the teams and technology, Domino's went from a struggling brand to an industry powerhouse. Their stock price surged from $2.82 to over $252 per share, adding roughly $12 billion to their enterprise value.

The key lesson you can learn from Domino's, as an AI-driven leader, is **technology is just a tool to achieve your goals. It is you as the leader who determines its impact. Strategy first. Technology second.**

In this chapter, we will cover change management strategies for smooth transitions. We'll cover five key steps to gain executive buy-in so you win support for AI initiatives. You'll learn that AI is a tool that delivers real value, never a solution looking for a problem We'll also talk about handling the common fears, misconceptions, and concerns that often accompany the adoption of new technologies. Let's dive in.

Gaining Executive Buy-In and Winning Support for AI Initiatives

Step 1: Identify the Problem

AI is just a tool; it is not the goal. Before you can try to win executive support for an AI use case, you have to be clear on the problem you are solving and if solving it will deliver business value.

Here are some questions you can ask yourself:

1. What are the organization's goals?
2. What are the key problems preventing progress toward our goals?
3. What do decision-makers care about most? (Where the focus goes, energy and money flows.)

Step 2: Identify The Use Case

From there, narrow your focus by qualifying potential use cases:

1. How might technology be a tool to help solve this problem?
2. Will this use case make an impact?
3. Are we confident we can get a win here?
4. What is the speed to value? Can we deliver fast wins, or will this take longer?
5. What's the risk if this use case fails?

Your goal is to identify high-impact use cases that align with business priorities, deliver quick value, create a strong first impression, and carry low risk.

Step 3: Map Stakeholders

With an idea of a potential use case, recognize that no one succeeds alone. You need executive support to get the approval and cross-functional support to embrace adoption.

This is where you have to map your stakeholders across the four groups we covered in chapter 9: decision-makers, influencers, champions, and early adopters.

Then there is you. You do not have to have a direct line to the decision-maker. You just need to find a champion who does. Ask yourself the following questions:

1. Who are the decision-makers?
2. Who are the people who could influence the decision-makers?
3. Who is the champion for this use case?
4. Who can represent the people who will be most impacted by the change?

For each person, you can also ask the following questions:

1. What does this person care about?
2. How might this use case support them getting what they care about?

Step 4: Co-Author Solutions

I have found that the best way to get support for a project is to have the people whose support you require co-author the solution with you. By making them a co-author, they feel a vested interest in seeing it through. Everyone loves their baby.

Here's how you do this. Based on your position in the organization, who is the one person you want to start with? Go to them with the problem you've identified, and engage them as a co-author in a potential solution.

Cast a high-level vision of the problem you've identified and how you perceive AI might be a powerful tool to solve it. Gauge whether there is interest or resistance. Invite the person to become an author of the solution so they feel ownership of it. From there, your job shifts to leading the execution.

Step 5: Lead Execution

When it comes to driving AI adoption within your organization, be clear on your role. Are you the decision-maker? An influencer? A champion? An early adopter? Or do you need to find someone who can champion your cause?

Regardless of which of these you identify with, since you are coming up with the idea, stay in the driver's seat leading execution. Make sure the ball keeps moving forward.

By following this framework, you will increase the odds that your AI use cases have strategic value and get the internal support required to get approved and funded. Remember, first impressions matter. Think big in terms of impact, and start small where you can get quick wins.

Create Support One Lightbulb Moment at a Time

If you want to create executive support, you need to help people have their own lightbulb moments so they think, "Wow! What else is possible?" To do this, ask them, "What's a challenge you are facing where you could benefit from having a Thought Partner?" When they give you an answer, turn to AI:

> I would like you to act as a Thought Partner by asking me one question at a time. Here's the situation: (provide the necessary context). Here's what I'm trying to solve: (then insert where you need help). Please help me think through potential solutions.

If you struggle to identify a moment where AI could help, ask AI to tell you.

> I am new to using AI and don't understand what it can do for me. I'd like you to interview me by asking one question at a time to identify something relatable in my work that you can help me do better.

Be Prepared to Address Concerns and Misconceptions about AI

As you champion AI within your organization, be prepared for mixed reactions. Referencing the adoption curve from chapter 3, recall that only 2.5% of your workforce are innovators and 13.5% are early adopters. This means a significant portion—84%—may not initially share your enthusiasm for AI and may have concerns and misconceptions about it. Anticipate these. When they arise, approach them with empathy and understanding. Here are strategic ways to navigate these challenges.

Validate Concerns

When concerns are raised, your job is not to make people feel like they are wrong. It is to acknowledge their concerns and validate them.

Here are some questions you can use to make this a productive discussion:

1. What might we gain from implementing AI in this case?
2. What do you think is the downside if we implement AI?
3. Based on this, do you think we should move forward and evaluate the impact? Or do you think this warrants pressing pause?

Asking these questions will get people out of an emotional state and help them think more strategically about AI. Engaging them in deeper discussions helps them feel heard, alleviates fear, builds trust, and fosters partnership in moving forward.

Now let's dive into specific concerns you might encounter, and how you can address them.

JOB DISPLACEMENT CONCERNS

Encourage people to think about their job as a combination of skills applied and processes followed. AI will augment or automate some skills and processes, but not all of them. Share your vision for how you believe AI's processing power can free them up to invest more time in higher-impact priorities. Be clear that their focus should be on developing the skills so AI can enhance them, not replace them.

It's important that you be transparent about what you know and what you do not know. What matters is leading with empathetic strength. AI is here, and it is not going away. Help your people adopt a growth mindset so they can evolve with technology.

DATA AND PRIVACY CONCERNS

Reinforce the organization's commitment to protecting data as a fundamental priority. Also acknowledge that there are solutions that can allow you to leverage generative AI while meeting the privacy and security needs of the business.

Considering how fast this technology is moving, I will not make specific recommendations here. We will keep an updated list of options on our website at AiLeadership.com.

REGULATORY RISK

You may be in an industry that has restricted the use of AI. In these cases, executives often hire attorneys to look carefully at what specifically is restricted. In one specific instance, leveraging artificial intelligence with customer data was prohibited, but the restrictions did not apply to their people leveraging it as a Thought Partner for content creation or marketing.

Depending on your situation, you can explore what is restricted and what is not. Then you can evaluate your willingness to explore from there.

RISK OF HALLUCINATIONS

Expect people to question whether they can trust the answers they get from AI. This is a valid concern. This is where you can walk them through the two roles: your role as the Thought Leader, and AI's role as the Thought Partner. When you get responses from AI, you can ask it to fact-check itself, as well as to cite sources.

Also recognize that the worst AI you will ever use is the version you are using right now. Since this is a generative product, it will continue to get better, and the hallucinations should decrease.

By listening and validating the concerns of your people, you then shift your focus to building momentum with your innovators and early adopters.

Empower Innovators and Early Adopters

Identify the innovators and early adopters within your company who are excited to explore AI's capabilities. Empower them by:

1. Giving them access to the right tools, such as approved large language models (LLMs), and guidelines on how they should and should not be used.

2. Offering training so they can get quick wins with AI.
3. Creating forums where they can collaborate and learn together.

Share Success Stories and Lessons Learned

Sharing success stories and lessons learned is critical if you want to create an innovative culture. The key is to get people talking. You will know you are successful when people share the wins they are having as well as the failures they've had and how they are refining their approach as they move forward. Once this flywheel is spinning, you know you are on the right track.

Ensure a Smooth Transition

Big changes start with small actions. As babies, we first crawl, then walk, then run. Your journey to AI adoption will follow a similar path. Cast a big vision for the impact this technology can make, and start with small use cases that can deliver fast value.

As momentum builds over time, you can expand adoption. Celebrate your successes, and learn from your failures. Remember, it's not the technology that will determine the impact; it's your leadership. Keep your people's interests at the center, and ethically adopt AI so it enhances them.

Now that you know how to integrate AI smoothly, let's move to the next chapter. We'll tie all the lessons from the book together and turn the big vision of *The AI-Driven Leader* into simple, actionable steps, helping you deliver real value with AI.

Here's the 20% from This Chapter

1. If you are wondering, Is my organization ready to adopt AI? The answer is yes.
   - Start small by increasing your productivity.
   - Then expand to helping your innovators and early adopters so the flywheel starts to spin.
   - Eventually you can consider using AI to increase operational efficiency and deliver more value to customers through innovative products and services

2. Strategy first; technology second.
   - Don't make AI a solution looking for a problem.
   - Start by identifying the problems that, if solved, would unlock business value.
   - Then identify the tools to help you unlock the value. AI is one of them.
   - Map stakeholders to win the executive support required. This includes your decision-makers, influencers, champions, and early adopters.
   - Change is hard, and people have fears and concerns. Your job is to lead with empathetic strength. You do this by listening and validating their concerns, maintaining a commitment to keeping people at the center of the business while still driving your company forward with AI.
   - AI adoption happens by consistently getting on base, not by swinging for the fences. Focus on use cases that are high impact with fast speed to value and have an acceptable level of risk. Create a good first impression and build momentum.

CHAPTER 14

Go from 0 to 1: The Simple Path to Deliver Value with AI

In 2004, Apple's iPod was more than just a gadget; it was a cultural icon. It revolutionized the way we interacted with music and raked in nearly a quarter of Apple's total revenue. The iPod had become Apple's golden goose.

But Steve Jobs was not one to bask in the glow of success. He understood that strategy is about building a competitive advantage in the long term through actions taken in the short term. While there were endless demands fighting for his attention that could have swallowed up his time, he knew he needed time to think.

His job as CEO was to look to the future, so he blocked out time to study market trends and anticipate potential threats. This disciplined approach allowed him to maintain a strategic edge. Perhaps he contemplated critical questions—such as what it would take to protect Apple's competitive advantage? What potential threats could challenge their revenue streams? And what actions could they take to ensure Apple's best years were ahead?

Regular strategic thinking helped Jobs develop the awareness to drive Apple forward. In doing so, he saw the rapid evolution of mobile phones and realized that they were quickly gaining capabilities that threatened the iPod's position in the market. Music playback, internet access, touch screen interfaces—features that were once the stuff of science fiction, were becoming standard in mobile devices. In contrast, the iPod, with its clicky wheel interface and its small, colorless screen, was starting to look increasingly outdated. He could imagine a world where these emerging technologies not only matched the iPod's capabilities but surpassed them, killing their golden goose.

Jobs knew he had to act, and fast. He assembled a team of Apple's top engineers, including Tony Fadell, Scott Forstall, and Jonathan Ive. Their goal? To create a revolutionary new device that would combine the functionality of a phone, internet device, and music player into one seamless product. This was no small task. The purpose of a goal is to inform who you can become, and in this case, their goal would require them to develop new touch screen technology, streamline the user interface, and integrate complex wireless capabilities. But they were up to the challenge.

On January 9, 2007, the world held its breath as Jobs took the stage at the Macworld conference. The air was thick with anticipation. For months, the tech community had buzzed with rumors and speculation. Industry insiders and the media had hinted at a major breakthrough, and enthusiasts speculated wildly online what the man in the black turtleneck and jeans might reveal.

Jobs began his keynote address with a bang. "Today we're introducing three revolutionary products," he announced. The crowd went wild. "A wide-screen iPod with touch controls. A revolutionary mobile phone. A breakthrough internet communications device." But then, Jobs dropped the bombshell. "These are not three separate devices. This is one device, and we are calling it iPhone."

The iPhone has become an indispensable tool, seamlessly integrated with our lives. It has fundamentally changed the way we work, navigate the world, access knowledge, and stay connected with one another.

The iPhone wasn't built in a day. **For Steve Jobs, it was the small action of prioritizing time to study the market that led to the awareness of a potential future threat. With that awareness, he was able to turn an existential threat into Apple's greatest opportunity. A decade later, Apple became the world's first trillion-dollar company.**

How might our phones look today if Steve Jobs had failed to prioritize time for strategic thinking? What would our work be like, or our interactions with family and friends? We'll never know. All history will recall is a creative genius who changed the world.

In life, it seems like there is always more to do than there is time. You know what it feels like to have endless demands competing for your attention. Days seem to fly by, leaving you wondering what you got done. You know you should be playing at a more strategic level, but it's tough to escape from the operational weeds.

The solution is simple, but it is not easy. It boils down to what you say yes to and prioritizing that. If you view your time as an investment, what return are those nagging demands giving you? What return could you get from strategic thinking and generating awareness?

Do you think Steve Jobs didn't face all the issues you face? There was an endless list of things he could have done. But he understood that his job as a leader was to build and fortify a competitive advantage. He didn't treat strategic thinking as a one-time event. Rather, it was a continuous process of asking big questions and generating awareness of future opportunities and threats. As a result, he surfaced opportunities others didn't see, which led to Apple taking actions others didn't take, and delivering results no one else did.

Building your competitive advantage in the long term starts with consistent strategic thinking time in the short term, and the first step is to move from 0 to 1.

Your Simple Path From 0 to 1 with AI

We've covered a lot in this book, but what's the simple path to go from 0 to 1? Remember how I interviewed over 200 leaders for this book?

- 100% of them believed AI was the future.
- 100% of them believed that their company would adopt it.
- Fewer than 5% had done absolutely anything.

Because most leaders are too busy with the current demands of their business, they don't understand what AI is, and they don't know where to start. No one has shown them the simple path to go from 0 to 1 to delivering actual value with AI. Let's make sure you're not one of them. So, here it is—the simple path from 0 to 1.

The AI Empowerment Flywheel

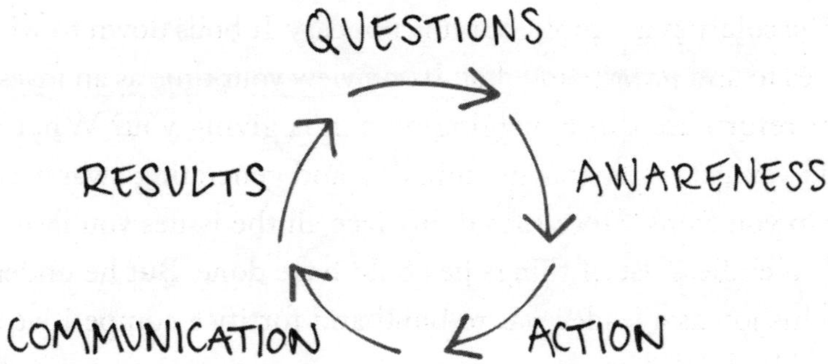

The AI Empowerment Flywheel represents your journey from 0 to 1. It starts with shifting the questions you ask yourself from "How might I do this?" to "How might AI help me do this?"

Right now, grab a sticky note and a Sharpie. Write **"How can AI help me do this?"** and place it on your desk. This simple step will keep AI top of mind and help you spot new opportunities to use it daily.

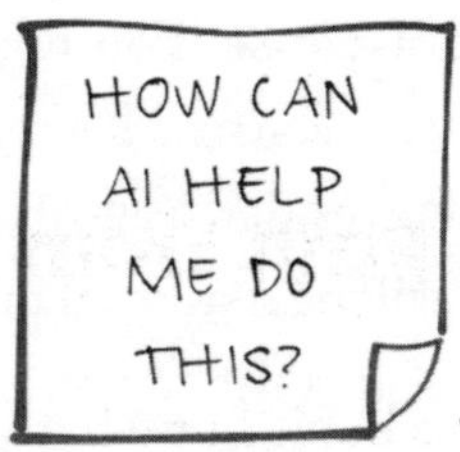

As you engage with AI, the quality of your communication will determine the quality of your results. The CRIT™ Framework will create quality results. Poor communication will create poor results.

This flywheel is what will drive you through the AI Empowerment Curve.

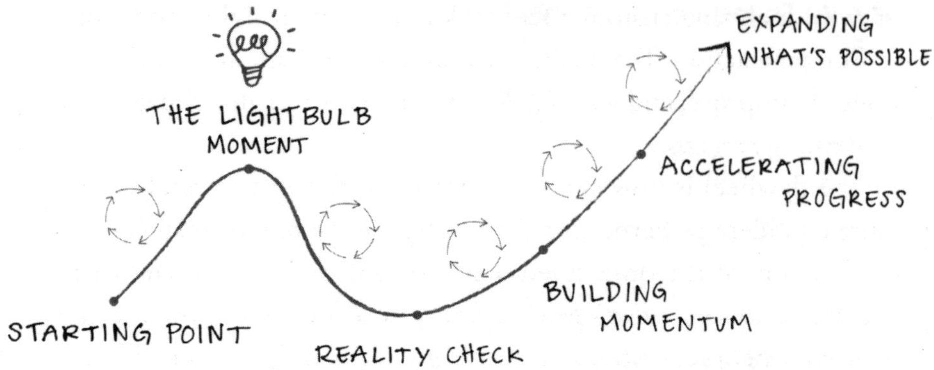

At the starting point, you are where you are. Ask the question, "How might AI help me do this?" This question will create awareness of a use case. You try using AI, and by communicating the context, role, interview, and task, you turn a relatable moment into a remarkable experience. Ding! You have *the lightbulb moment*.

Feeling excited about what AI might be able to do, you decide you are going to try this again. You ask, "How might AI help me do this?" You create awareness of a use case. You take action by engaging AI. The problem is, you have not learned how to communicate with AI yet. So you get poor-quality results. You hit *the reality check*.

By now you know this will be a normal part of your journey and do not let it discourage you. You stay the course by asking, "How might AI help me do this?" You create more awareness of situations where you can try AI. You take action, but this time you focus on using high-quality ingredients in your communication like CRIT™. You get higher quality results and you start *building momentum*.

You keep asking, "How might AI help me do this?" but now you are expanding it across a larger set of use cases: strategic thinking, decision-making, content creation, idea generation, analysis, and research. You create greater awareness—thinking through a performance review for an employee, making a decision on resource allocation, creating messaging for investors, identifying potential strategies to drive faster growth, analyzing customer feedback to generate insights, and more.

You take action. The quality of your communication with AI continues to improve, and you continue to get better results. You are now *accelerating progress.*

The flywheel is now spinning faster and faster, and you become more confident in harnessing AI to help you do higher-quality work in a fraction of the time. Eventually, you will get to the stage where you are *expanding what's possible*, and you will wonder how you can help your people, systems, and culture become AI-driven. That is when I want you to ask "How might AI help me do this?"

Expanding Your Use of AI: A Simple 3-Step Framework

Over time you will expand your use of AI across much of what you do. Here is a simple three-step framework to help you go from 0 to 1 in any situation.

1. **Ask AI to Interview You:** Don't know how to use AI for a situation? Ask AI to interview you to identify a way it can help in one of the specific categories listed above. Let AI help you identify something you need to tackle this week where it can add value.

   Here's the prompt:

> Please interview me by asking one question at a time to find a way you can assist with (insert category) that I need to tackle this week.

2. **Generate a High-Quality Prompt:** Once you've identified something you need to do this week that you think AI can help with, ask it to generate a high-quality prompt tailored to that need. Also, request an explanation of why it structured the prompt that way.

   Here's the prompt:

> Please create a high-quality prompt for that. Also please explain why you structured it the way you did so I can learn how to write great prompts from you.

This step not only provides you with a powerful tool but also helps you understand the logic behind effective AI prompts.

3. **Execute the Prompt:** Once you have a good prompt, tell AI to execute the prompt it generated.

> Great. Now please execute that prompt so you can help me accomplish this task.

This will allow you to see the AI work as your Thought Partner to deliver the result. Remember, the first response you get may be directionally correct but still fall short of what you need. Give it feedback on what you like and don't like so it can refine its answer for you. You are the Thought Leader. AI is your Thought Partner.

By following this three-step framework, you will quickly go from 0 to 1 in harnessing AI across different use cases.

Ready to Apply What You've Learned?

For a quick training to help you apply these concepts, visit AiLeadership.com/start. Access my crash course and go from 0 to 1 today.

As you experience AI helping you do higher-quality work in a fraction of the time, you will naturally want to drive this through your organization. My intention in this book was to present a simple path to AI adoption in a way that will bring value. I also want to be clear. Just because something is simple does not mean it is easy.

You know that driving change throughout an organization is not easy. Even the smallest behavior changes can require herculean effort to scale across your organization. AI is different from implementing a new SAAS platform or company policy. We're talking about shifting the way people work by rewriting decades of habits people have formed to help them become AI-driven. The truth is, you and your people are always forming habits. The question is, are they conscious or unconscious?

It was the unconscious habits that were being formed among Domino's employees that led to the crisis in the late 2000s. Turning that ship around required challenging everything from their pizza recipe to the way pizza was ordered by the customer to how it was delivered. Patrick Doyle's vision for quality pizza that was easy to order and fast to deliver was one thing. But turning that vision into reality required getting people on board. They had to invent new systems. Then they had to conduct lots of training with franchisees, with clear standards for compliance and support. This was not "another thing to do." It was the top priority that warranted relentless focus and execution—and it drove $12 billion in enterprise value. Surely it wasn't easy, but it was worth it.

AI adoption might be simple, but simple is rarely easy.

The Challenges Ahead

AI is simple. Changing how your organization is structured is the hard part.

Most leaders get stuck here. They believe AI is the future, and they have the intelligence and ambition to make it work. The problem is that the way their organization operates was built for a slower world. That gap is being exposed every day.

What used to be small inefficiencies are now critical failures. What used to cost you time now costs you position. And what used to be manageable is quickly becoming unsustainable.

Speed to value is the new competitive advantage. And most organizations are losing.

The challenges I'm about to walk you through are showing up inside companies every day. If you look closely, you may see them inside your own.

Challenge 1: The Speed Gap

You've had the meeting. The priorities are clear, the team is aligned, and there's energy in the room. Two weeks later, nothing has moved, or worse, different teams have moved in different directions.

Decisions take too long. Alignment starts to fade. Execution slows as priorities continue to shift. The momentum you built dies before it ever turns into results.

It's not that your strategy is wrong. It's that your organization can't turn strategy into results fast enough.

You are competing on speed to value, and right now your company is not built for it. While you're spending time trying to drive alignment, your competitors are executing. They're deciding while you're discussing. They're learning and adapting while you're still planning. Over time, that gap compounds—and it becomes increasingly difficult to close.

Challenge 2: The Leadership Gap

Every organization says AI is a priority. But here's the real question: are your leaders actually leading it?

Great leaders lead by example. They don't just talk about change, they model it. And in most companies, that's where things are breaking down.

We hear so many executives say the organization needs to become AI-driven, but they haven't yet made the shift themselves. If you followed them around day to day, you wouldn't see them consistently using AI to elevate how they think, make decisions, or create value. The commitment sounds strong, but in practice, it starts to fracture. The truth is, they are more interested than they are committed.

So what happens? AI gets pushed down into the organization. Every team is told to explore it. A few tools get tested. Some use cases get identified. Meanwhile, leadership continues to operate the same way it always has, the way it thinks, the way it makes decisions, the way it runs the business. Nothing fundamentally changes.

And when leadership doesn't change, the organization doesn't change either.

This creates a deeper problem. Leaders lack the vision to see what's truly possible and the credibility to lead others there. They are asking their teams to transform the way they work while they still operate the way they always have. It becomes a "do as I say, not as I do" dynamic, and people feel that.

Here's the uncomfortable truth: you cannot build an AI-driven organization without AI-driven leaders. You have to transform the leader before you can transform the organization.

If leadership doesn't change how it operates, AI will remain an experiment. Your momentum will stall and your transformation will never happen. And while you are hesitating, your competition is making progress.

Get in the driver's seat and lead by example. It is your job to become an AI-driven leader.

Challenge 3: The Alignment Breakdown

Ask five leaders on your team what the top priorities are for the organization. How many of them would give you the same answer?

Misalignment rarely shows up as conflict. It shows up as quiet friction. Your team is working hard, but they're not always working on the right things. As a result, initiatives overlap, compete, and start to stall.

You see constant rework because expectations weren't clear. Decisions get revisited because people weren't truly aligned in the first place. It starts to feel like progress, but it's not. Your people are busy, but are they actually effective? Are they delivering results?

Misalignment is the silent killer of speed. It slows execution, frustrates teams, and causes you to miss opportunities that should have been captured. And in a world where speed matters more than ever, you can't afford that drag.

This isn't about identifying a list of AI use cases. The real opportunity is using AI to align the efforts of your team so you can achieve more than you ever thought possible.

Challenge 4: The Strategy Execution Gap

Most organizations don't have a system that ensures their strategy actually turns into results.

They rely on meetings to drive alignment, tools to manage work, and the heroics of individual leaders to push execution forward. But there's no integrated system that keeps everyone aligned on what matters most and ensures that every person is taking focused action with clear accountability as priorities evolve.

As a result, things fall through the cracks. Priorities shift, but people aren't always clear on what changed or where they should focus. Teams stay busy, but they're not always moving in the same direction. And when that happens, it becomes difficult to hold people accountable—not because they aren't working, but because they're not always sure what target they're aiming at.

In a slower world, you could get away with this. Today, you can't. AI is accelerating the pace of change, and most organizations are not built to keep up. You cannot use an outdated way of operating to win in an AI-driven world.

The result is predictable: the gap between you and faster-moving competitors doesn't just exist, it gets wider.

These aren't four separate problems. **They are symptoms of one deeper issue: your organization is trying to operate in a new world using an old way of working.**

That is why progress feels slower than it should, and opportunities feel harder to capture. It's also why AI feels promising, yet doesn't consistently deliver results.

If you want different results, you don't need another tool. You need a different way of leading your team.

In the final chapter, we'll break down the key takeaways from this book and, more importantly, I'll share my top solution to help you overcome these obstacles, so you can turn AI from a promise into a competitive advantage.

CONCLUSION

Redefine Who You Are and Who You Can Become

Ever since we were kids, we've been asked, "What do you want to be when you grow up?"

The problem with this framing is that it focuses on what you want to do professionally, not who you want to become. As a result, many people mistake what they do for who they are. This gets to the heart of why so many people are afraid of AI—not because they fear losing their job but because they fear losing their identity.

Here's the truth: You are you, not what you do. You were born to grow and evolve. It's woven into your DNA. The challenge is, part of your brain sees change as a threat. It sees change as the death of your current self and makes you want to resist it. Don't. Embrace it.

As you evolve from 'leader' to 'AI-driven leader,' you will shift what you do. You will change the way you work, the tasks you focus on, and the way you invest your time. But—and this is crucial—that does not change who you are. Because you are you, not what you do.

My hope is that your experience does not end with this book, but with you becoming an AI-driven leader who builds a better business and better lives for your people. The question to ask is, who can you become?

Only you can provide the answer.

AI is not coming—it's already here. The difference between those who thrive and those who fall behind will not be defined by access to AI tools, but by how you think and lead your team forward.

This book has not just been about AI. It has been about you—your leadership, your thinking, and the choices you make that will define your future. In order to lead in this new era, you must shift from reacting to AI to shaping its role in your business. This requires evolving from an operational leader to an AI-driven leader—one who harnesses AI as a strategic Thought Partner, not just a tool.

The world is changing faster than ever before. **You can either lead that change or be disrupted by it. The choice is yours.**

Key Takeaways from Each Chapter

Chapter 1: The Rise of AI and the AI-Driven Leader

- AI is not just another technology shift—it is reshaping how decisions are made, businesses operate, and leaders think.
- Leaders who fail to adapt risk irrelevance. Those who embrace AI gain an unfair advantage.

Chapter 2: We've Been Here Before

- Your job = (skills you apply) × (processes you follow).
- Technology will change the skills you apply and the processes you follow. Adopt a growth mindset and use AI to enhance you, not replace you.

Chapter 3: Shift from Operational Overwhelm to Strategic Clarity

- AI-driven leaders do not get stuck in day-to-day operations—they use AI as their thought partner to think strategically.
- Your job is to think, not just execute. AI can handle the low-level tasks, but you must stay in the driver's seat as the Thought Leader, defining your vision and leading your team.

Chapter 4: Understand AI

- There are three ways AI can bring value: it can make your people more productive, your operations more efficient, and your products and services more valuable.

- There are three skills you need to develop: the ability to identify strategic use cases, communicate effectively with AI, and stay in the driver's seat as the Thought Leader.

Chapter 5: Supercharge Your Leadership

- AI is just a tool. Your ability to harness it as a leader is the difference that makes the difference. Think strategy first, technology second.
- The top use cases include:
    - Strategic Thinking
    - Decision-Making
    - Content Creation
    - Idea Generation
    - Analysis

Chapter 6: The High Price of The Wrong Questions

- Great leaders aren't the ones with all the answers. They're the ones who ask the right questions.
- Ask strategic questions that are aligned with your goals, are simple and clear, and provoke deeper thinking.

Chapter 7: Collapse the Time from Data to Decisions

- AI allows leaders to make better decisions in minutes, not months.
- Previously, data analysis required waiting weeks for results from an analytics team. Now, AI provides answers in seconds.

Chapter 8: Navigating Short-Term Pressures Without Sacrificing Long-Term Growth

- The pressure to deliver immediate results often leads to sacrificing long-term growth priorities. Giving in to this pressure breaks the chain between your actions today and your competitive advantage tomorrow.
- AI can help you align your actions in the short-term with your competitive advantage in the long-term.

Chapter 9: Accelerate Strategic Momentum

- To make faster, smarter decisions follow the strategic decision-making framework:
- Clarify the objective
  - Map stakeholders
  - Gather and analyze information
  - Identify solutions and alternatives
  - Evaluate risks
  - Decide and plan implementation
  - Deliver results

Chapter 10: Lead With Strategic Clarity

- The purpose of a goal is not to achieve a result. It's to act as a compass, informing who you can become.
- Clarity and alignment are not permanent. The moment you assume you have it is the moment you start losing it. Revisit your plans often and engage your AI Thought Partner™ to expand your thinking.

Chapter 11: Win The First 30 Days

- The actions you take in the first thirty days can make or break your goals. Get out of the gates fast, and build a lead in your first thirty days.
- Break your plan down into small, actionable steps and have time blocked on your calendar to take those actions.

Chapter 12: 10X The Impact of Every Employee

- Harness the strengths of a person, focused on the priorities of their role, aligned with company goals, and use AI to enhance them, not replace them.
- Set the standard that people own 100% of their job. That includes thinking leverage.

Chapter 13: Integrate AI Seamlessly

- AI adoption is a leadership challenge, not a technical one.
- Success depends on clear communication, team alignment, and the right cultural shifts.

Chapter 14: Go From 0 to 1

- Big changes start with small actions. Grab a sticky note and a Sharpie, and write: "How can AI help me do this?"
- Then, once a day, every day, for the next 30 days, write a prompt following the CRIT™ Framework: Context, Role, Interview, Task.

Take the Next Step

You now have the framework to become an AI-driven leader. The question is simple: what will you do with it?

Most leadership teams are facing the same reality. You know AI matters, but you're not using it to transform how you think, make decisions, and lead. You've identified dozens of AI use cases, but you're not seeing the value you expected.

It's not because the use cases are wrong. It's because you haven't transformed how you think as a leader. If your leadership team hasn't become AI-driven, it's easy to chase use cases instead of focusing on what actually drives growth—aligning your people on what matters most and executing against it at AI speed.

And while you're working to figure that out, the world is moving. Competitors are deciding faster, adapting faster, and pulling ahead.

That's the gap.

This is the work we do every day. We work directly with your executive team to transform how you think, make decisions, and lead as AI-driven leaders—so you can lead the transformation, not delegate it. Most companies start here.

From there, we help you move faster by collapsing three to six months of alignment into a matter of hours and installing an AI-driven strategy execution system that turns your strategy into results.

Every voice is heard, decisions that used to stall for months get resolved, and your team leaves clear, aligned, and ready to execute on what matters most.

If this is how you want your organization to operate, it's time to act. Visit AiLeadership.com.

This Is for You If:

- You know AI needs to be driven from the top and you want your senior leaders to lead by example.
- You know your company needs to move faster, but alignment keeps breaking down across teams and functions.
- You understand this is about leadership transformation, not just adopting new technology.

This Is NOT for You If:

- You're looking for AI hacks or tools rather than a leadership transformation.
- Your organization is unwilling to change how leadership operates.
- You want to wait and see what happens rather than take control of how AI reshapes your business.

If this resonates, visit AiLeadership.com to learn how we can help you transform the way you lead your company.

The leaders who win with AI will be the ones who can turn strategy into results the fastest. We would love to help you become one of them.

Your Journey Begins

You have an incredible opportunity to let go of the way things used to be and reimagine the way things can become. By becoming an AI-driven leader, you are joining a new category of leaders who are taking a stand for a new way of working. Together, we are moving away from outdated industrial methods that required us to set aside our humanity to meet the needs of machines. Together, we are moving toward a future where we harness our strengths, focused on the priorities of our roles, aligned with our company goals, and use AI to enhance us, not to replace us.

This is my vision for the future. Will it come true? I believe so. My invitation to you is to use this book to discover who you are and who you can become. Harness your unique strengths at work, and use AI as a tool to build a better business and better lives. This is the journey of becoming an AI-driven leader.

Who can you become? The answer lies within you.

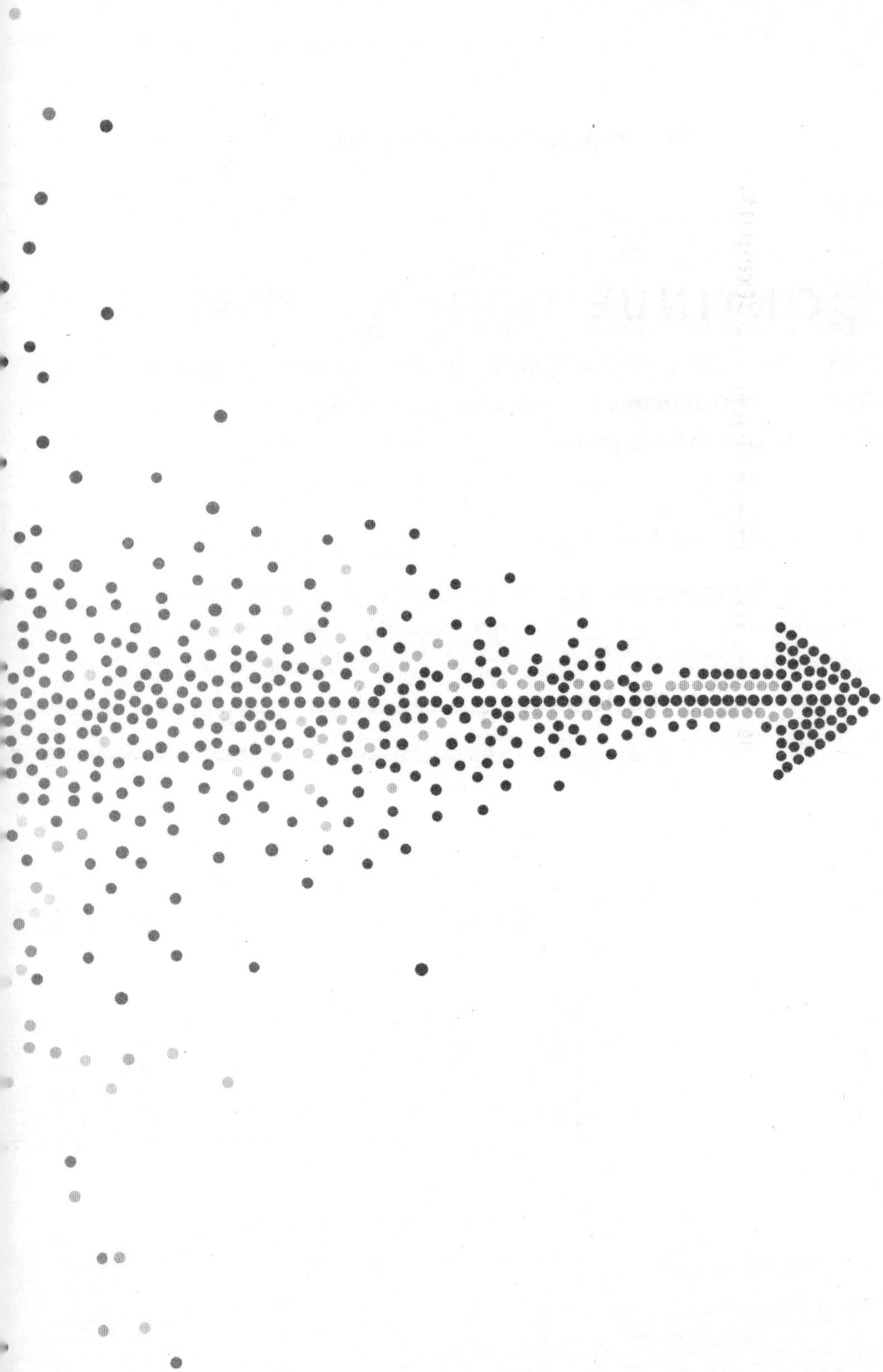

CONTINUE YOUR JOURNEY

The following resources are available
to you to help you become an AI-Driven Leader:

1. Becoming an AI-Driven Leader Executive Training
2. Speed to Alignment Executive Sessions
3. AI Thought Partner™
4. The AI-Driven Leader Podcast
5. AI Leadership Newsletter

Visit www.AiLeadership.com

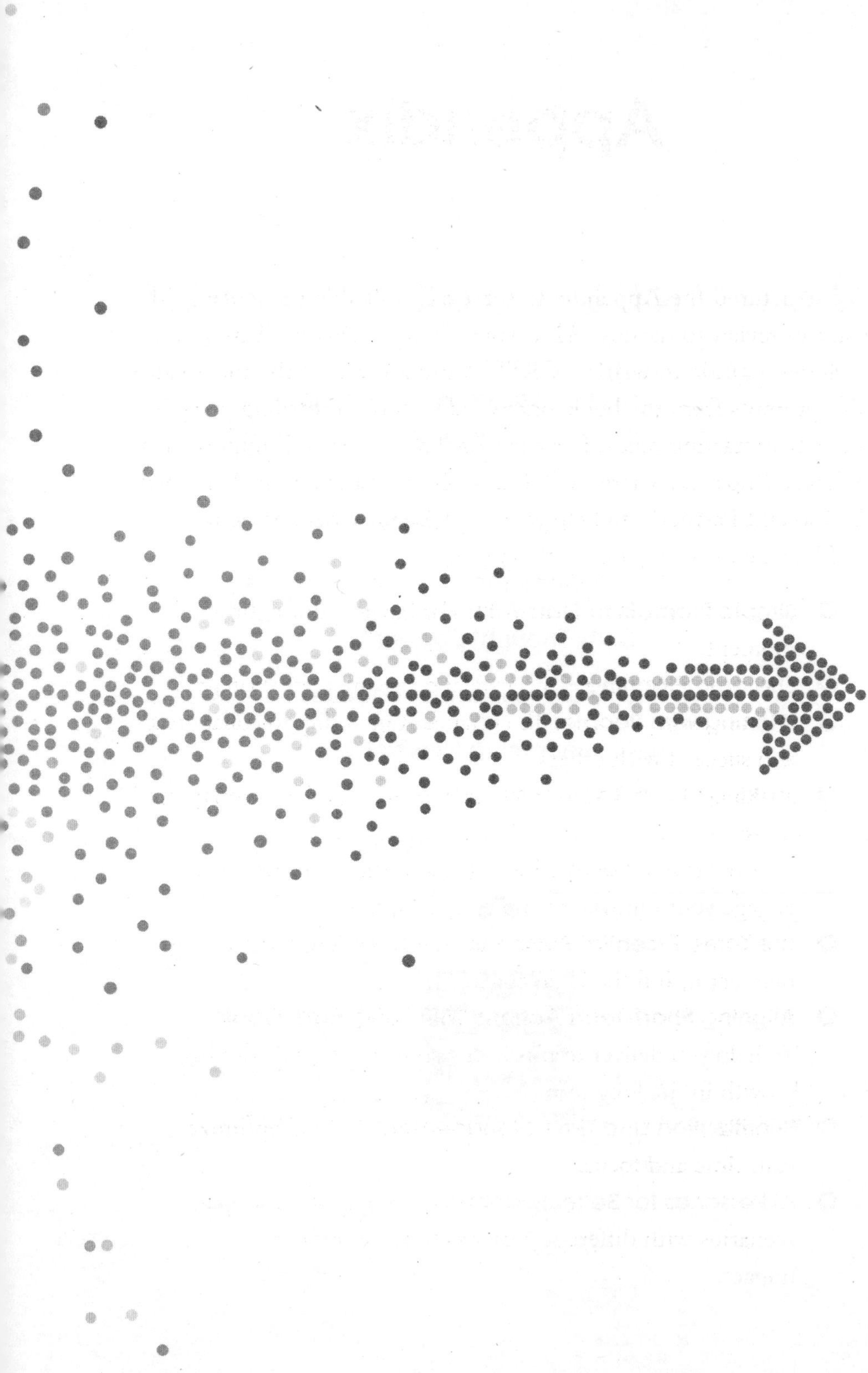

Appendix

I've structured the Appendix to serve as a valuable reference guide you can revisit to harness AI as your Thought Partner. This section includes a guide to writing CRIT™ and a recap of the most valuable prompts from the book, organized by topic, providing you with a practical starting point. For additional resources and support, visit AiLeadership.com, where you'll find more tools and our finely trained AI Thought Partner™ to help you put these prompts into action.

Here are the categories of the prompts:

- **Simple Prompts to Start With:** For having your lightbulb moment.
- **Strategic Planning:** To clarify and execute your strategy.
- **Winning with People:** To enhance your ability to collaborate and succeed with others.
- **Making Great Decisions:** For improving the decisions you make.
- **Clarify Your Vision and Build Momentum:** To help you engage your innovators and early adopters.
- **The Three Essential Personas:** The Interviewer, the Communicator, and the Challenger.
- **Aligning Short-Term Actions With Long-Term Goals:** To help you deliver results in the short term while driving growth in the long term.
- **Prioritization and Time Management:** So you optimize your time and focus.
- **AI Personas for Better Feedback:** To help you role-play scenarios with different personas to increase your impact.

- **Prompts from Company Case Studies:** To recap of the actual prompts companies used to get results.

How To Write CRIT™

CRIT™ is simple to learn and powerful in practice. Here is exactly how to use it.

Step 1: Set Up the Structure

Open your AI tool and type the following headers in all caps, pressing Shift + Return three times between each one so they stand apart:

CONTEXT

ROLE

INTERVIEW

TASK

This gets the architecture into the context window. From here, you simply fill in each section.

Step 2: Fill In Each Section

CONTEXT is where you describe the situation you are dealing with in detail. The more you give, the better your results. Do not edit yourself. Use speech-to-text if you can. When you type, you tend to self-correct and trim. When you talk, you give AI the full picture. AI can handle unorganized thoughts. More is better.

ROLE is where you describe the expert you want advising you. Go beyond generic. Instead of "act as a marketing expert," try:

> You are a world-class CMO with deep expertise in health and wellness. Your superpower is identifying what marketing teams have done historically and determining what AI can do better, while keeping human insight at the center.

The more specific the role, the sharper the result.

INTERVIEW should always read:

> Interview me. Ask me one question at a time, up to three questions, to gain deeper context.

Every word here is intentional.

1. "Interview me" tells AI to ask instead of answer.
2. "One question at a time" turns it into a conversation. Without this instruction, AI will flood you with questions at once.
3. "Up to three questions" sets a limit. Three questions will be sufficient 80% of the time. If you want to go deeper, push to four or five. I do not recommend going beyond five.

TASK is where precision matters most. Aim AI at the wrong target and you will not get what you need. One of my favorites:

> Based on this, give me the top three high-impact, non-obvious strategies I should deploy to solve this problem.

Three keeps the list focused. High-impact filters for the 20% that drives 80% of results. Non-obvious is critical. Without it, there is a risk AI will confirm your existing thinking and tell you what you want to hear. Non-obvious forces it outside the box.

Step 3: Refine the Result

The first response is just a draft, not the answer. Stay in the driver's seat.

1. Tell it what you like.
2. Tell it what you do not like.
3. Tell it the top changes you want it to make.

This is what separates leaders who get good results from leaders who get great ones.

Step 4: Stress Test the Answer

Once you are happy with the result, do not stop there. Ask AI to switch roles:

> Now I want you to act as the Challenger. You are world-class at stress testing the insufficiency of a plan. Tell me what you like about this, what you don't like, and the top changes I would need to make to ensure this plan is bulletproof.

Then watch what happens. AI will shift from partner to critic — surfacing the blind spots, the weak assumptions, and the gaps you could not see because you were inside the box. This is where good plans become great ones.

Simple Prompts to Start With

IF YOU WANT TO USE AI AS A THOUGHT PARTNER BUT DON'T KNOW WHERE TO BEGIN

> I'm curious to explore using you as a strategic Thought Partner. I'd like you to interview me by asking one question at a time to identify a simple and valuable use case where you can help me clarify my thinking this week. Then continue interviewing me to help me clarify my thinking.

CREATE YOUR LIGHTBULB MOMENT

> I would like you to act as a Thought Partner by asking me one question at a time. Here's the situation: (provide the necessary context). Here's what I'm trying to solve: (then insert where you need help). Please help me think through potential solutions.

Strategic Planning

ANALYZE YOUR STRATEGIC PLAN 1

> Attached is our strategic plan. I want you to act as my Thought Partner by asking me one question at a time to challenge my biases and the assumptions we have made. I also want you to challenge if our plan has the sufficiency to achieve our goal. Once you have enough information, give me a summary of where you think our plan is strong and where you see potential weaknesses, and recommend ways we can improve it.

ANALYZE YOUR STRATEGIC PLAN 2

Help me evaluate my current strategic plan. What are the strengths, potential weaknesses, and areas for improvement based on emerging market trends and internal capabilities?

ENGAGE AN EXECUTIVE COACH TO CHALLENGE YOUR ASSUMPTIONS ON A STRATEGIC PLAN

Take a look at our strategic plan for our upcoming fiscal year. Acting as an executive coach, I need you to challenge our assumptions. Start by questioning our goals: are we really pushing the envelope, or are we playing it safe? Then assess the structure of our plan: is it robust enough to achieve our goals even when things don't go as planned, or are we too reliant on ideal conditions? After our discussion, I'd appreciate your feedback on the strengths of our plan, areas for improvement, and actionable advice to ensure we're set up for success.

ESTABLISHING YOUR REVIEW RHYTHM

I'm the leader of a (describe your business). We just completed our strategic off-site where we created our strategic plan for the year. I now want to establish a rhythm where we will review our plan to ensure we track our progress and realign on what we need to execute moving forward. Acting as a growth-minded operations expert, please help design this review rhythm. Start by identifying up to three questions you want to ask me to gain additional context, and then ask them one at a time. Then generate a draft of the review rhythm. I'll provide feedback from there.

CONDUCT YOUR STRATEGIC REVIEW

Act as my Thought Partner and interview me with one question at a time to conduct a quarterly strategic review of my business. The questions should focus on these four drivers:

1. **Strategy:** What competitive advantage are we building in the long term through the actions we are taking in the short term?
2. **Execution:** What progress have we made toward our strategic plan so far this year? What changes do we need to make?
3. **People:** Are the right people in the right seats doing the right things and growing in the right direction?
4. **Technology:** How might we harness technology to help our people do higher-quality work in a fraction of the time, increase efficiency, and deliver more value to customers?

Start with strategy and continue through each driver in order. Then give me feedback on what I'm doing well and where you see potential holes in my thinking, and list the top things I should consider focusing on in the next ninety days.

DOUBLE REVENUE IN TWENTY-FOUR MONTHS

Our goal is to double revenue in the next twenty-four months to become an attractive acquisition target. Attached is our strategic plan. I want you to act as a strategic growth expert by helping me identify non-obvious alternatives we could consider to drive this growth. You can ask me up to five questions to gather what you need about my business. Once you have sufficient context, give me your recommendations listed in order of priority and explain why you are making each recommendation.

DRAFT A BUSINESS CASE

I need your help creating a business case for an initiative to increase the productivity of our employees across our organizations.

For context, we are (insert company details).

I want you to structure the business case around the following sections:

1. What We are Trying to Do and Why it Matters
2. How It Will Impact the Organization
3. What the Implementation Plan Looks Like
4. What Investment Will Be Required
5. What the Risks Are and Plans to Mitigate Them
6. What Our Next Steps Are

Please interview me, asking me one question at a time, to pull the necessary information out of my head so you can then create a draft of this business case. Once you have enough information, generate the business case following the structure above.

ENGAGE A DEVIL'S ADVOCATE ON YOUR STRATEGIC PLAN

Attached is our strategic plan for the next fiscal year. Acting as the Devil's Advocate, review our plan and ask critical questions that could expose flaws in the plan's ability to achieve our overall goal. Please prepare a detailed report evaluating the strengths and weaknesses of our strategy, and offer recommendations to improve.

Winning With People

EVALUATING TEAM SKILLS WITH COMPANY GOALS

I want you to help me evaluate the current skills and capabilities of my team against the goals we have. Interview me by asking one question at a time to gather the information you need. At the end, give me a summary of where you think we are well positioned and where we have gaps and the top three actions I should consider taking.

PREPARE FOR A STAKEHOLDER MEETING

I need to prepare for an upcoming stakeholder meeting. Please interview me by asking one question at a time to help me create an agenda for the meeting. Once we have the agenda, then prepare the communication I can send to set expectations for what to expect.

RECAPPING A PERFORMANCE REVIEW IN WRITING

> I just concluded a performance review with an employee. After writing the follow-up email, I realized it comes off as too harsh. I need it rewritten to be clear on expectations and maintain firm performance standards but also be empathetic and softer so the employee receives it well. Below is the original email; please regenerate it based on this description.

RAISE YOUR STANDARDS ON THINKING LEVERAGE

> I am an executive within our company. I have a leader who tends to come to me for answers, and I've noticed that I get frustrated because the things they ask they should be able to handle themselves. I want you to act as a world-class executive coach in helping me identify five potential questions I could ask this person the next time they come to me without doing their own thinking first. Avoid questions that are overly direct. I want the person to feel like I'm supporting them while holding a standard.

HOW TO SAY NO TO YOUR BOSS

> I want your help as an executive coach who is an expert in prioritizing and effectively saying no to new requests, especially when they come from the boss.
>
> #Context#
>
> My boss has a tendency to constantly put more things on my plate. I already feel spread thin and need to find an effective

way to talk to them about what's on my plate. I want to be "in the driver's seat" of my role and be able to communicate what my priorities are with confidence. I also want to be able to speak to how maintaining focus on my top priorities will add the most value to our team. As a result, I need to ask that certain things they have delegated to me be tabled or reassigned.

#Your task#

Is to ask me one question at a time to better understand the situation and then give me some potential ways I can have this conversation. Once we review your recommendation, I'd like to role-play this situation with you. Just ask me some questions about my bosses personality so you can accurately role-play as them.

Making Great Decisions

EVALUATING TWO OPTIONS

I need to make an important decision. I'm considering these two options. Your task is to evaluate the upside and downside of each potential solution and explain which you'd recommend and why.

IDENTIFY POTENTIAL RISKS

I need to make an important decision. Here is the situation: (describe the situation). Here are the solutions I have identified so far: (list the solutions you've identified). I want you to act as an expert in identifying risk and help me see the second-order consequences of these solutions.

ANTICIPATE OUTCOMES

> I need to make a strategic decision involving (describe specific situation). Can you help me analyze the potential outcomes of different options based on our historical data and predicted market developments?

RESPOND TO A CRISIS

> We are facing a crisis involving (describe the crisis). I need to formulate an immediate action plan. Can you guide me through the process of risk assessment and the development of a response strategy?

EVALUATING RISK

> I need to make an important decision. Here is the situation: (describe the situation). Here are the solutions I have identified so far: (list the solutions you've identified). I want you to act as an expert in identifying risk by asking me one question at a time to help me see the second-order consequences of these solutions.

Clarify Your Vision and Build Momentum

CLARIFY YOUR VISION FOR AN AI-DRIVEN ORGANIZATION

> I want you to act as my Thought Partner in helping me create a vision statement around AI, outlining:

1. How I believe it will benefit our company
2. How I see it benefiting our people
3. Where I see potential risks with AI and how we can work together to manage it

Interview me by asking one question at a time. Once you have enough information, generate a draft of what I might share with other people.

IDENTIFY AND INVITE A FIRST ADOPTER

I want to identify someone on my team to join me in exploring adopting AI in our daily work. Interview me, asking one question at a time, to identify a person who is innovative, growth-minded, and influential. I want this person to become a champion of change.

Once we have the person identified, role-play with me. You will act as them, and I will present my vision for our future and the benefits they might experience by joining me in exploring this.

At the end of the conversation, give me feedback on what I did well, where I have opportunities to improve, and the top changes I can make to increase the quality of my message.

IDENTIFY KEY STAKEHOLDERS

I need to make a decision for our business and want to be strategic about involving the right people in the process. Acting as my Thought Partner, I want you to interview me by asking one question at a time to help me answer the following questions:

1. Who are the decision-makers who can approve or reject this decision?
2. Who are the influencers who can sway the thinking of the decision-makers I need to engage?
3. Who are early adopters who will be most affected by the decision because they are closest to the point of impact?

Then, help me analyze what each person cares about and how the decision impacts them. This will help me communicate the benefits and mitigate potential downsides.

Structure your answer in a table format.

The Three Essential Personas

ENGAGE THE INTERVIEWER

I want you to act as the Interviewer by asking me one question at a time to (describe what you want AI to learn from you). Based on the feedback I give you, I want you to (describe the task you want it to complete).

Example: I want you to act as the Interviewer by asking me one question at a time to understand our current marketing plan. Based on the feedback I give you, I want you to identify three non-obvious growth levers we should be considering but are not currently in our plan.

ENGAGE THE COMMUNICATOR

We are launching a new product (describe the product). Act

as The Communicator to help me craft a compelling pitch that highlights our product's unique features. Interview me by asking one question at a time. Once you have enough information, craft the pitch.

ENGAGE THE CHALLENGER

I want you to act as the Challenger. Your job is to stress test my thinking to make sure I'm not only seeing the upside but that I also see the downside and non-obvious second-order consequences. Ask me one question at a time to challenge my thinking. Start by asking me to describe the situation.

Aligning Short-Term Actions With Long-Term Growth

OPTION 1

I need your help balancing short-term results with long-term growth. I want you to review our strategic plan, then interview me to help me identify what will deliver the most long-term value and where we can deliver quick wins that will keep the board happy while we invest in the future.

OPTION 2

I want you to act as a strategic Thought Partner in helping me reevaluate if our short-term actions are aligned with our long-term vision. Please interview me to help think this through, and give me feedback on where my thinking is solid and where you see areas for improvement.

OPTION 3

> I am an executive looking to ensure that what I am focusing on in the short term not only helps us achieve our goals this year but is also in alignment with our long-term goals.
>
> Act as my executive coach and ask me one question at a time to:
>
> 1. Understand our long-term goals.
> 2. Understand what I am prioritizing in the short term.
> 3. Evaluate if I am focusing on the right things in the short term to achieve our long-term goals.

> Please help me identify any potential blind spots and prioritize my actions to stay on track.

Prioritization and Time Management

ANALYZE IF YOUR CALENDAR IS ALIGNED WITH YOUR PRIORITIES

> Here are my top priorities for this week. Here is also a picture of my calendar for the week. In reviewing my calendar, I don't feel it reflects a clear plan to achieve my weekly goals. Acting as the Interviewer, ask me one question at a time to help me identify changes I can make to the calendar.
>
> Once we're done with the review, I want you to help draft the communication I need to send to the people I'm canceling or rescheduling.

ENHANCING THE VALUE OF YOUR ONE-ON-ONES

Acting as my Thought Partner, help me identify three to five questions I can bring to my next series of one-on-ones with my direct reports. My goal is to act as a great coach, focusing our conversation on:

1. Ensuring they are clear on where their focus needs to be this week to drive progress toward our thirty-day milestones.
2. Helping them think through the challenges they might encounter this week and how to proactively address them.
3. Raising their performance this week so they continue to develop and grow.

Ask me one question at a time to gather the information you need, and then generate a list of questions for me to consider.

TURNING YOUR STRATEGIC PLAN INTO THIRTY-DAY MILESTONES

Attached is our strategic plan. The next step is to identify the specific progress we need to make for each item on the plan in the next thirty days to be on track for our targets. Ask me one question at a time to help gather this information, then generate an executive summary communication I can send to my team so we are aligned.

HOW TO COMMUNICATE PRIORITY CHANGES TO MY PEOPLE

I am the leader of a business. Historically I've delegated to people by simply adding but rarely having conversations about subtracting. As a result, I'm concerned people are reacting to what's most recent, and losing focus on what's most important.

I'd like you to act as an executive coach by asking me one question at a time to help me think through how I might change what I say and ask when I delegate. Success would be describing what I need them to take on and then more of the conversation focusing on where they believe this falls in order of priority. This will ensure they do not react and always stay focused on what matters most.

EXECUTE: TURN MONTHLY GOALS INTO WEEKLY PRIORITIES

Attached is our strategic plan for the year. To be on track for this plan, I need to accomplish the following things this month: (list your monthly goals).

Your job is to act as an executive coach to help me identify what I can accomplish this week to start building a lead toward my monthly goals. Please ask one question at a time. Also make sure to adhere to a SMART goal framework, and prioritize my list.

LEVERAGING AI TO ASSESS THE IMPACT OF NEW PRIORITIES ON THE EXISTING PLAN

Attached is our strategic plan. Recently, there has been pressure to (describe the new priority). I'd like you to act as a strategic Thought Partner in helping me assess the impact of this new priority on the existing plan. Ask me one question at a time, and respond based on my answers.

IDENTIFY YOUR 20%

I want you to act as my Thought Partner to help me identify how I can 10x the impact I can make for my organization. My intention is to harness my strengths, with the priorities of my role, in alignment with the company goals.

Your task is to ask me one question at a time to:

1. Clarify the 20% priorities of the business based on our strategic plan (attach if you have it).
2. Identify the 20% priorities our business goals require my role to do exceptionally well.
3. Help me uncover my 20% strengths that drive 80% of the value I can deliver.

Based on the information you gather, help me understand the intersection between my strengths, the priorities of my role, and the company goals.

AI Personas for Better Feedback

SIMULATING YOUR IDEAL CUSTOMER REVIEWING YOUR PROPOSAL

I want you to act as our ideal customer, (describe your customer), in reviewing the attached proposal. Simulate how they might respond by providing me with feedback on:

1. What you like about our proposal.
2. What you do not like about it or things that may not make sense to you.
3. The top changes we can make to ensure this proposal is something you would agree to.

SIMULATING A BOARD MEMBER REVIEWING YOUR STRATEGIC PLAN

I want you to act as a growth-minded board member and review our strategic plan. What questions or potential concerns do you have based on our deck? Put a focus on ensuring we are striking the right balance between short-term execution and long-term growth.

SIMULATING A BOARD MEMBER REVIEWING YOUR BOARD DECK

I want you to act as an aggressive growth-minded board member with deep expertise in company turnarounds. Attached is the board deck for this business. It's not doing well and needs to be turned around. I'd like you to identify the top five questions that you would be asking the CEO during this meeting. Please list them in order of priority, as we only have one hour for the review, and I want to make sure I'm asking the most important questions first.

ANALYZE A PRODUCT OFFERING BASED ON YOUR IDEAL CUSTOMER

> I want you to act as an ambitious non-technical executive of a growth company. Here is an idea I have for a product offering: (then I describe the product). Here's the problem I believe it solves and the benefits it will bring: (describe the problem and benefits). My goal is that you will see this solution and think, "This is exactly what I need!" Your goal is to tell me what you like about my idea, what you do not like, and the top changes I should consider making. Offer solutions as well and explain why they are important to you.

ROLE-PLAY AS A KEY STAKEHOLDER

> Role-play with me as if you are the decision-maker. I'll present a recommendation for your approval, and I want you to simulate their likely response. Challenge me where they might resist so I can practice my responses. Afterward, provide feedback on:
>
> 1. What I did well.
> 2. Where my approach was not strong enough.
> 3. The key changes I can make to increase my odds of success.

Specific Prompts that Companies Used

ROLE-PLAY AS A POTENTIAL CLIENT

> I am an executive with a consumer packaged goods company.

We have a meeting coming up with the CEO of Whole Foods. Our goal is to gain strategic alignment as a preferred partner.

Your role is to research Jason Buechel, the CEO, and identify what matters most to him in a partnership.

Now act as Jason Buechel, the Whole Foods CEO, in reviewing the attached presentation against the six priorities you've outlined.

Please structure your response highlighting:

1. The strengths of our presentation.
2. What we are missing.
3. What we can do to improve.

DATA-DRIVEN INSIGHTS

We are a steel manufacturing company. Attached is our order book history for the last three years showing production by product by plant. I've also attached our sales projections for this upcoming year showing the same. This includes assumptions we have made on what production might look like by product at each plant. Acting as the Analyst, please review the data to identify underlying trends to validate or challenge our assumptions.

SERVE AS A BRANDING AGENCY

You're a brand designer for bestselling authors. Your task is to create my brand colors and provide hex codes for each. My topic is AI-driven leadership, and I want to be thought of in the same light as Simon Sinek, Jim Collins, and Peter Drucker. My target audience is executives who are innovative and ambitious and who have decision-making authority to implement projects and allocate capital (for example: founders, CEOs, chief strategy officers, CIOs, and the venture funds that fund them). I also want you to generate the following for my brand specifically: our core values, the brand voice, our target audience, brand colors, fonts, and fashion that I would wear. Please generate three options.

FLORIAN USING AI TO EVALUATE A TRAINING PROGRAM FOR BAYER INDONESIA

#CONTEXT#

I'm an executive with a large multinational organization based in Indonesia. We're going through a reorg where up to 20% of our management will leave. This will cause the management layers to flatten. As a result, leaders cannot operate with a command-and-control style of leadership. They must empower their people to think strategically and make decisions independently in alignment with the business goals.

I'm recognizing that there will be skill gaps specifically in strategic thinking, decision-making, and storytelling. We need training programs for these. My initial thought was to use AI to build the curriculum internally.

I perceive this will save us on cost and create an opportunity for internal champions to have a vested interest in the content and be more bought in.

(continued)

#YOUR ROLE#

Is to act as a strategic Thought Partner to complete the following tasks:

1. Highlight the strengths and weaknesses of AI when it comes to designing the curriculum and writing it so it has high-quality relevance and is focused on active learning.
2. What are the alternatives I should consider to create an upskilling program?
3. Identify benchmarks where AI has been used to help create internal upskilling curriculum and if it was successful. Cite your sources so I can check.

Acknowledgments

Family

Amy: You have always supported me in my ventures. I could not have asked for a more supportive partner. I love you so much.
Daphne, Dean, and Aspen: You inspire me. I'm proud to be your dad.
Mom and Dad: For being a great example of what love can look like. You always supported me and encouraged me to focus on who I was becoming and trying my best. I love you.
Lauren: For a great childhood and putting up with me as your brother.

Team

Charlie Hoehn: You have been my guide through this whole process. This book would not be what it is without you and your support.
Carly Sandstrom: For staying in the driver's seat and keeping me focused on this book.
Ann Maynard: For your help making things pop.
Pete Garceau: For turning my vision into an amazing cover.
Valerie Brown: For your wonderful images.
Zoe Norvell: For making the interior stand out.
Brady Wilkin: For your contributions to the book.
AJ Hendrickson: For catching the little things.
Marianella Pintos: For being my right hand in expanding what's possible.
R. Joe Ottinger: For your friendship and thought partnership.
Vaughan Stanford: For your friendship and leadership in AIL.

Special Thanks

To the 200+ leaders I interviewed for this book: You know who you are. You helped shape this. Thank you.

Jay Papasan: For teaching me how to think.
Gary Keller: For teaching me to think bigger.
Naveen Jindal and the Jindal family: For putting your trust in me and creating a life-changing opportunity to work with your businesses and see the world. This is where my AI journey began.
To my Front Row Dad brothers: It's an honor to go on the journey of being family men with businesses, not businessmen with families.
Jason Bronstad: For your friendship and support.

Those Who Have Supported Me on My Journey (Alphabetical Order)

Aayush Arora: For the conversations we shared and your enthusiasm for what I do.
Abhinav Kohli: For our conversations and your help bringing the use case to life.
AK Pandey: For being coachable and trusting me to guide you.
Allan Young: For the interview and connections.
Andrew Kuhn: For your friendship and the connections.
Andy Malk: For making me feel welcome and showing me what a connector looks like.
Ann Higgins: For our conversation and your enthusiasm.
Ben Laws: For facilitating the moment that shaped the conclusion.
Bethany McDaniel: For your vision, trust, support, and your love of pranks.
Bimlendra Jha: For our conversations business and spiritual.
Blake Mallen: For your partnership and collaboration. The future is bright.
Bob Minford: For your trust, support, and being a champion of change.
Brian Scudamore: For your guidance and friendship.
Brooke Fernandez: For the interview and enthusiasm.
Carlos Cortina: For your collaboration and leadership.
Chad Johnson: For your coaching and friendship.
Chantell Preston: For your energy and enthusiasm about my direction.
Chris Edelen: For the interview and connection to Frank.
Chris Taylor: For the fridge and creating a space where great entrepreneurs can connect.

Chris Winton: For our friendship and the opportunities you've created.
Craig Joyner: For being a powerful influence in my life.
Cody Foster: For your support and friendship.
Damodar Mittal: For always smiling.
Damon Frier: For helping me see that the path in front of me was not the best path for me.
Dan Krug: For our time together and the conversations we have shared.
Dave Meltzer: For your mentorship and guidance.
David Armano: For reminding me of the responsibility I had in writing this book.
David Robshaw: For your leadership in creating an AI-driven company.
Deb Borg: For your collaboration and thought partnership.
Don Ho: For your perspective and helping make the book better.
Doug Tatum: For reinforcing this book's direction.
Drew Little: For your friendship and encouragement.
Ed Nottingham: For your support and being a champion of positive change.
Ekhlaque Bari: For your collaboration and contributions.
Eric Fraser: For the conversations and your contribution to chapter 4.
Erik Frywald: For your guidance, support, and early advocacy of AIL.
Florian Zirnstein: For being coachable and sharing your story.
Frank Iannella: For your story and support of the book.
Frank Krazovec: For a great conversation and trusting me with your network.
Gene McNaughton: For your mentorship and guidance. You helped me think bigger when I felt stuck.
Greg Reid: For opening the door to a whole new world of people.
Greg Shove and the Section Team: For helping me go from 0 to 1.
Grady Davis: For your collaboration. We are going to do some amazing things together.
Hanan Wajih: For opening the door and your partnership.
Harssha Shetty: For being coachable and a great leader.
Indra Datta: For our conversations on AI.
Jared Cruce: For our conversations and sharing use cases.
Jayce Fitch: For our long friendship.

Jayme Hoffman: For challenging me to interview 100 customers. That challenge shaped this book.
Jenny Wall: For reinforcing the direction I have been on.
Jeremy Utley: For the conversations and collaboration.
Jim Bunch: For your friendship, guidance, and expanding my mind.
Jim Franzen: For our conversations.
Joe Riesberg: For contributing your perspective to this book.
Jon Vroman: For starting FRD and supporting me in becoming a family man with a business
Justin Barton: For being a life-long friend.
Justin Donald: For your friendship and support over the years.
Justin Levy: For our long friendship and the motivation.
Karan Sandhu: For my "lightbulb moment" and our friendship.
Katie Boes: For a great conversation and your contributions to the book.
Keith Cunningham: For teaching me the value of thinking time.
Konrad Szczepanik: For your friendship and our worldly experiences together. LET'S GO!!!
Kurt Wilkin: For the connections to great people.
Laura Haggarty: For getting in the driver's seat and leading change in AIC.
Leesa Soulodre: For sharing your experience.
Madhumita Ray: For making my time in India so smooth.
Mark Bula: For trusting me and going deep.
Matt Cherish: For challenging me to ask, "What are the skills I can master that are so valuable they will serve me no matter where I go?"
Matt Gottlieb: For our lifelong friendship and the braccos.
Matt Neuman: For our conversations and the partnership.
Melissa Mullady: For your ongoing friendship, support, and belief in what I do.
Michelle Epps: For your trust and support.
Mike Lauderdale: For being the most entertaining HR executive I know. Your feedback was real and helped shape this book.
Mike Smirklo: For sharing your perspective and welcoming me into your community.
Nik Petrik: For taking action in your company and the support.
Paul LeMay: For your real feedback and helping make sure the book

delivers the results I intended.
Paul Saganey: For our relationship and the opportunities that lie ahead for us.
Pooja Shah: For the relationship and the conversation.
Rich Horner: For taking me under your wing.
Rick Heitzmann: For your perspective and contribution.
Robin Ross: For our friendship and your collaboration.
Ryan Moran: For being a great friend and supporting me on my journey.
Ryan Trontz: For our friendship.
Sabyasachi Bandyopadhyay: For trusting me and the real conversations. You are a good man.
Sanjeev Dixit: For your collaboration.
Sanjeev Gupta: For our conversations and time in Africa.
Scott Emery: For your support in my entrepreneurial ventures.
Scott Galloway: For your ideas and starting Section.
Shane Driggers: For helping shape our direction.
Seth Streeter: For great conversations and your support.
Sitikantha Pattanaik: We made a great team.
Steven Sorrells: For helping me realize the problem leaders are facing.
Stephan Gratziani: For your partnership. The universe brought us together for a reason
Subham Singh: For being coachable and your support.
Sudhanshu Saraf: For helping me find "my next level." You helped me be better at what I do.
Tanner Luster: For your friendship, leadership, and support.
Tim O'Sullivan: For bridging the gap to what's possible.
Tim Sharp: For a great story.
Travis Bonner: For pushing me to be better and showing what standards can look like for performance.
Tuff Yen: For your valuable feedback and perspective.
Velveth Schmitz: For your contributions and energy.
Whitney Knight: For your partnership in bringing this to your organization.
Wyatt Graves: For your friendship and support, and for being the first member of The Collective.
Zack Lofton: For your support and applying what you've learned.

Geoff Woods is the #1 bestselling author of *The AI-Driven Leader*, host of The AI-Driven Leader podcast, and Founder of AI Leadership, where he helps organizations turn strategy into results in a fraction of the time by installing AI-driven execution systems.

As the former Chief Growth Officer of Jindal Steel & Power, Geoff's strategic leadership helped the company grow its market cap from $750 million to over $12 billion in just four years. Prior to that, he co-founded the training and consulting company behind The ONE Thing, advising businesses ranging from $10 million to $60 billion in annual revenue.